READ AND RESPOND

A Course in Creative Reading

Lionel Jackson
Moray House College of Education
Edinburgh

Mary Jackson
Scottish Centre for Education Overseas
Moray House College of Education
Edinburgh

HODDER AND STOUGHTON

LONDON SYDNEY AUCKLAND TORONTO

Note to Teachers and Students

Reading is a creative act. It is not just a matter of decoding a text. To read well we must bring our experience to the text to create meaning and understanding. What we know and feel become ingredients in the reading process. We may enjoy, disagree with, be amused or surprised by what we read. Often we can refine or extend our response by talking, listening or writing. In fact the four modes of English are interdependent.

This approach to reading is reflected in the layout of this book. The passages will appeal, it is hoped, to most readers in their mid-teens and above, inviting them to reflect and respond. The questions aim to help this process.

Question 1 a focuses on a few key points in reading for meaning, linking them with our own lives.

Question 1 b considers more detailed points of language and meaning for students interested in a more analytical approach.

Question 2 offers suggestions for talking and listening, usually on a group basis.

Question 3 invites the reader to write, imaginatively or from experience, on the theme of the passage.

Words in **bold** type in the questions are explained in the glossary, which will thus offer the student a range of language concepts met in context. The questions are guidelines, not interpretation exercises. Teacher and students, working together, may wish to select, rephrase and make up their own questions, explore unexpected paths or digress, according to the pool of experience of the whole group. Some students will be able to tackle some questions without help but often the teacher will be coach or consultant, aiding and advising the individual or the group in their efforts to master the arts of reading, talking, listening and writing.

The passages, covering a wide range of style and content, are grouped under broad themes, which may prove useful for unit studies. Other, related materials, particularly poems, will readily suggest themselves. For example, Wole Soyinka's 'Telephone Conversation' could be read alongside *Black Like Me* and 'Tam O' Shanter' with *Witches*. Students should be encouraged to find other relevant materials.

Contents

* These passages may be found more difficult in style or content

1 Thank You, M'am
Langston Hughes

This story about two black people in the USA is by a Negro writer.

She was a large woman with a large purse that had everything in it but
a hammer and nails. It had a long strap, and she carried it slung across
her shoulder. It was about eleven o'clock at night, dark, and she was
walking alone, when a boy ran up behind her and tried to snatch her
purse. The strap broke with the sudden single tug the boy gave it from   *5*
behind. But the boy's weight and the weight of the purse combined
caused him to lose his balance. Instead of taking off full blast as he
had hoped, the boy fell on his back on the sidewalk and his legs flew
up. The large woman simply turned around and kicked him right
square in his blue-jeaned sitter. Then she reached down, picked the   *10*
boy up by his shirt front, and shook him until his teeth rattled.

After that the woman said, "Pick up my pocketbook, boy, and give
it here."

She still held him tightly. But she bent down enough to permit him
to stoop and pick up her purse. Then she said, "Now ain't you   *15*
ashamed of yourself?"

Firmly gripped by his shirt front, the boy said, "Yes'm."

The woman said, "What did you want to do it for?"

The boy said, "I didn't aim to."

She said, "You a lie!"   *20*

By that time two or three people passed, stopped, turned to look,
and some stood watching.

"If I turn you loose, will you run?" asked the woman.

"Yes'm," said the boy.

"Then I won't turn you loose," said the woman. She did not release   *25*
him.

"Lady, I'm sorry," whispered the boy.

"Um-hum! Your face is dirty. I got a great mind to wash your face
for you. Ain't you got nobody home to tell you to wash your face?"

"No'm," said the boy.   *30*

"Then it will get washed this evening," said the large woman,
starting up the street, dragging the frightened boy behind her.

He looked as if he were fourteen or fifteen, frail and willow-wild, in
tennis shoes and blue jeans.

The woman said, "You ought to be my son. I would teach you right   *35* from wrong. Least I can do right now is to wash your face. Are you hungry?"

"No'm," said the being-dragged boy. "I just want you to turn me loose."

"Was I bothering *you* when I turned that corner?" asked the   *40*
woman.

"No'm."

"But you put yourself in contact with *me*," said the woman. "If you think that that contact is not going to last awhile, you got another thought coming. When I get through with you, sir, you are going to   *45*
remember Mrs. Luella Bates Washington Jones."

Sweat popped out on the boy's face and he began to struggle. Mrs. Jones stopped, jerked him around in front of her, put a half nelson about his neck, and continued to drag him up the street. When she got to her door, she dragged the boy inside, down a hall, and into a large   *50*
kitchenette-furnished room at the rear of the house. She switched on the light and left the door open. The boy could hear other roomers laughing and talking in the large house. Some of their doors were open, too, so he knew he and the woman were not alone. The woman still had him by the neck in the middle of her room.   *55*

She said, "What is your name?"

"Roger," answered the boy.

"Then, Roger, you go to that sink and wash your face," said the woman, whereupon she turned him loose – at last. Roger looked at the door – looked at the woman – looked at the door – *and went to the*   *60*
sink.

"Let the water run until it gets warm," she said. "Here's a clean towel."

"You gonna take me to jail?" asked the boy, bending over the sink.

"Not with that face, I would not take you nowhere," said the   *65*
woman. "Here I am trying to get home to cook me a bite to eat, and you snatch my pocketbook! Maybe you ain't been to your supper either, late as it be. Have you?"

"There's nobody home at my house," said the boy.

"Then we'll eat," said the woman. "I believe you're hungry – or   *70*
been hungry – to try to snatch my pocketbook!"

"I want a pair of blue suede shoes," said the boy.

"Well, you didn't have to snatch *my* pocketbook to get some suede shoes," said Mrs. Luella Bates Washington Jones. "You could of asked me."   *75*

"M'am?"

The water dripping from his face, the boy looked at her. There was a long pause. A very long pause. After he had dried his face, and not knowing what else to do, dried it again, the boy turned around, wondering what next. The door was open. He could make a dash for it   *80*
down the hall. He could run, run, run, *run!*

2

The woman was sitting on the daybed. After a while she said, "I were young once and I wanted things I could not get."

There was another long pause. The boy's mouth opened. Then he frowned, not knowing he frowned.   85

The woman said, "Um-hum! You thought I was going to say *but*, didn't you? You thought I was going to say, *but I didn't snatch people's pocketbooks*. Well, I wasn't going to say that." Pause. Silence. "I have done things, too, which I would not tell you, son – neither tell God, if He didn't already know. Everybody's got   90 something in common. So you set down while I fix us something to eat. You might run that comb through your hair so you will look presentable."

In another corner of the room behind a screen was a gas plate and an icebox. Mrs. Jones got up and went behind the screen. The woman   95 did not watch the boy to see if he was going to run now, nor did she watch her purse, which she left behind her on the daybed. But the boy took care to sit on the far side of the room, away from the purse, where he thought she could easily see him out of the corner of her eye if she wanted to. He did not trust the woman *not* to trust him. And he 100 did not want to be mistrusted now.

"Do you need somebody to go to the store," asked the boy, "maybe to get some milk or something?"

"Don't believe I do," said the woman, "unless you just want sweet milk yourself. I was going to make cocoa out of this canned milk I got 105 here."

"That will be fine," said the boy.

She heated some lima beans and ham she had in the icebox, made the cocoa, and set the table. The woman did not ask the boy anything about where he lived, or his folks, or anything else that would 110 embarrass him. Instead, as they ate, she told him about her job in a hotel beauty shop that stayed open late, what the work was like, and how all kinds of women came in and out, blondes, redheads, and Spanish. Then she cut him a half of her ten-cent cake.

"Eat some more, son," she said.   115

When they were finished eating, she got up and said, "Now here, take this ten dollars and buy yourself some blue suede shoes. And next time, do not make the mistake of latching onto *my* pocketbook *nor nobody else's* – because shoes got by devilish ways will burn your feet. I got to get my rest now. But from here on in, son, I hope you will 120 behave yourself."

She led him down the hall to the front door and opened it. "Good night! Behave yourself, boy!" she said, looking out into the street as he went down the steps.

The boy wanted to say something other than, "Thank you, m'am," 125 to Mrs. Luella Bates Washington Jones, but although his lips moved, he couldn't even say that as he turned at the foot of the barren stoop

3

and looked up at the large woman in the door. Then she shut the door.

From *Third World Voices for Children*

―――――――

1   a   (i)   Which of your own experiences comes nearest to that of the boy *or* the woman?
           (ii)   What is interesting about the woman's name?
          (iii)   Do you have more sympathy with the boy or the woman?
          (iv)   Look again at lines 64–85. Is the boy telling the truth when he says he snatched the pocket book in order to get blue suede shoes?
          (v)   Why does Mrs Jones make the boy wash his face?
      b   (i)   Explain what we mean if we say that this story is **fiction** but based on **fact**.
          (ii)   Say why **italics** are used at certain points in the story.
          (iii)   Mrs Jones says that 'shoes got by devilish ways will burn your feet' but she does not mean it **literally.** How would you **interpret** what she says?

2   a   This is a **dramatic** story with interesting **dialogue**. In groups, discuss how all or part of the story could be tape-recorded. Would you need a **narrator**, or sound effects?
      b   Decide what the boy does with the ten dollars he receives (about £10 today) and improvise the talk he has with his mother later in the day.

3   'I have done things, too, which I would not tell you, son – neither tell God, if He didn't already know.'
        Write a short piece describing Mrs Jones at work the next day, thinking about past events.

2 Young People
Mav Franks

It's ridiculous – this 'us' and 'them' attitude that many older women seem to have towards teenagers (that very word a horrid Americanism). If we lived up to the horrific image they seem to have of us, we would all be dashing round in screaming hordes beating up old grannies for their pensions. The day would be punctuated by occasional jabs from a hypodermic. Night time would be greeted by leaping into bed with the first person we suspect is of the opposite sex, as they reckon you can't tell these days.

Usually I'm quite indifferent to the so-called teenage problems, being nineteen myself and thoroughly bored with the whole thing. But I go to an evening class where I'm the only young person and the place seems to take on the character of a battlefield where I cower in the corner under a constant shower of bullets of accusation and disapproval. These ladies run down my contemporaries right, left and centre, ask my opinion and then don't give me time to have a proper say. So now's my chance.

Last week they were all very anxious about drugs because most of them have teenage daughters. They asked me if I'd ever been offered drugs. I said yes, I'd tried marijuana a few times, and they were all very shocked. Yet it was quite some while ago, and because of this experience, I now know that I don't need drugs and that they hold no real attraction for me.

These things are blown up by publicity and anxiety, to be so large, but we have freedom of choice, and we have to work through these things and often come out of it better off ultimately for the experience. All the telling in the world doesn't make any difference, we have to find out for ourselves, just as my children and the children of my contemporaries will and as you did in the past.

Another question was 'Why are young people so immoral?' But surely it depends what you call immoral. I want to know why the word immoral is always linked with sex. Maybe we do act differently as far as boy-girl relationships go but this is just another part of growing up. We have to find out for ourselves.

I don't think young people want to isolate themselves from older people but some older people isolate themselves from us by narrow-mindedness and lack of adaptability. My father, when he sees an unconventional film on television just complains violently. He's clinging to the past and has stopped growing up. He thinks it isn't his world anymore although he's living in it. Why grow up? Why ever grow up? I don't want to.

You can't imagine how super it is to talk to an older person and feel that they're the same age as you. And it isn't because they've degraded themselves to becoming phoney teenagers like these swinging vicars. It's because they've kept open minds, young minds. They're learning all the time and admit they can learn from the   45
young, just as we learn from them. I think it unfortunate that these open-minded people are usually men because the poor mums are often housebound, and have to think about their husbands' meals, school kids' new shoes and endless cups of tea. But really I think none of this matters if people just observe.   50

When most people think of a paving stone, they think it's grey; but if they bothered to observe they would be surprised by all those colours before their eyes. Sometimes it's necessary to re-learn to separate noises and smells and feelings, to observe all those things   55
you don't even bother to notice in a day, to awaken those senses that have become so sleepy.

The world is so beautiful and it belongs to all of us, not to any group, and anyway how can you put people into groups? We all have different ages just as we have *different* personalities. I've met   60
fifty-year-old twenty-year-olds, just as I've met twenty-year-old fifty-year-olds. So I say break down the barriers and let's try to understand each other. Let's listen to each other for a change instead of shouting each other down. Let's rid our minds of all these prejudices that can make life for some so unbearable and fill them   65
instead with *knowledge* and understanding and appreciation of all the million things around us. They're there just waiting to be absorbed to make our conversation livelier, our faces brighter, and our smiles wider.

I have a friend who would like to see us all dance in the streets   70
everywhere we go, as in *West Side Story*. I think it's worth considering.

From *Woman's Hour: A Second Selection*

---

1 a   (i) What does 'this "us" and "them" attitude' mean?
       (ii) 'All the telling in the world doesn't make any difference, we have to find out for ourselves' (ll. 26–27). From your own experience, say what this 'telling' might include.
       (iii) Do you agree that the author's father 'has stopped growing up' (l. 38)?
       (iv) What are 'phoney teenagers' (l. 43), 'swinging vicars' (l. 44) and 'fifty-year-old twenty-year-olds' (l. 61)?

(v) Do you agree that 'these open-minded people are usually men because the poor mums are often housebound' (ll. 46–48)?

(vi) The last three paragraphs introduce a new idea. Can you say what it is?

b   What clues can you find in the **language** of this piece, taking into account both the speaker's purpose and her audience, to suggest that it was a broadcast talk?

2   The author asks 'why the word immoral is always linked with sex' (ll. 30–31). In your groups discuss how you would answer this question.

3   Write a letter from a thirteen-year-old girl *or* a fifty-three-year-old man to Mav Franks, commenting on her broadcast and asking some questions. Then write the letter Ms Franks might send in reply.

3 The Cow
Neil Gunn

Like the other members of the family she had a name: Nanz. She
was a big Ayrshire cow, sleek, with sides bulging like a great cask and
with a wonderful nose for a tasty bite. She was condemned with
affection as the best scrounger in the district. And one evening in
particular she gave him a fright. For some reason he had been late and   *5*
when he reached the park he found that all the cattle had been driven
home. The park was empty. He went beyond it to unfenced braes near
the sea, but she was not there. From gleaned information, he went
beyond the braes to the cliff-heads. It was a long way and fear was in
him now. It was so easy to fall over the cliffs that neither cattle nor   *10*
sheep were allowed there.

He climbed up over the Head, keeping well back against the dry-
stone dyke that separated the top fields from the cliffs. At first the
distance between the dyke and the cliff-edge was fairly broad but soon
it narrowed to a mere passage way and then he saw her in front, the   *15*
dyke on her left side and the sheer drop on the other, revelling in a
growth of rare succulence.

At once the boy stepped back lest she see him, for he instinctively
realized that he mustn't frighten her now. She knew she was doing
wrong. She knew she would be for it. A wild swing round or a barging   *20*
on, and she might finish at the foot of the cliff. Out of her sight, he
climbed over the dyke and noiselessly went forward in its shelter until
he had got well beyond her. His heart was beating strongly and he was
feeling a bit sick, for the height of a cliff could get inside him. Then
carefully he climbed and put his head over the dyke. She saw him and   *25*
her head swung up. She looked at him steadily, a thing she rarely did.
She stopped munching, with the grass sticking out of her mouth. They
might have been strangers meeting in very remarkable circumstances.

"Go on now," he said.

"Moo," she said.   *30*

"Home," he said, keeping the conversation up as best he could.
She had another tear at the grass and lifted her head.

"That's enough," he said. "Go on now." His voice firmed.

She began to go about, backing her haunches towards the dyke, her
head over the brink; then she was round and walking away. A   *35*
weakness of relief went over him. He kept inside the wall, following
and exhorting her, until the passage broadened and she was clear.
Then he climbed the wall and came in behind her. He had her now!
The time for payment was not yet. Over the root of the Head, and now
the descent of the steep brae. He hung back, giving her time. Once a   *40*

hind leg slid and she sat down, but she never lost her balance, heavy as she was. There was no denying she was wise. He even told her to take her time. Take your time, you fool! In his anxiety, he encouraged her strongly until she was down on the level and then he told her that she was in for the greatest hiding of her life. He even stole forward to give *45* her as foretaste one wallop with the small stick he had picked up. But she knew him and got out of reach, and then he saw something that stopped him for as her udder swung from side to side milk streams came from the teats.

She was so full, she couldn't hold any more. Wasn't it like her! But *50* the milk remained in his mind.

At long last the byre, the chain fixed round her neck, and she was at his mercy. He picked up the hoe, prepared to belabour her with its handle. His whole evening had been ruined, she might have killed herself. *55*

"Ah, you!" he said and gave her a wallop on the haunch. She stepped about the cobbles and swung her tail.

"That will learn you," he said, "not to go to the cliff heads!" And he gave her a second wallop.

She swung her head, looked at him and gave a double switch with *60* her tail as if there were a lot of flies about.

"Ah, you!" he said and half-raised the hoe, leaving her to understand that she was very lucky not to be given a third blow.

"Maybe you'll remember that!" he added powerfully, putting the *65* hoe away.

"Hooo," she said, still trying to whip flies.

He was surprised to find afterwards that though there were head-shakings about that encounter on the cliff, still he had done something that might not have been expected of his years, something even *70* remarkable. He could read the look in an eye, the suppressed smile, and even his mother's grave face had something behind that he wasn't supposed to see but that he saw. If anything can be subtler than a boy's insight into elderly attitudes it is his vanity. But alas, the rare, comforting, swelling feeling of vanity wasn't given a long life in that *75* milieu, not even supposing you tried to hang on to it and at the same time blow it still larger, like a soap bubble at the end of a clay pipe, by discounting the importance of the incident. Och it was nothing! His elder brother got the whole story out of him, including what he had hitherto suppressed, the almighty thrashing he gave to the cow in the *80* byre. This was the final, the grown-up touch.

"Boy, I fairly gave it to her!" he said, feeling very big.

"What did you do that for?"

"Why not? She needed it, didn't she?"

"But she would have forgotten by that time what it was for." *85*
There was a pause then. "She would not! She knew fine!"

His elder brother laughed. "She would. Nanz is just a cow. She would have forgotten."

"She isn't! She would not!"

"She would so."

"She would not!" *90*

His brother laughed.

A burst soap bubble is cold even on the hand. For he saw that Nanz may not have understood. It spoiled everything.

From *The Atom of Delight*

1　a　(i)　How old you think the boy is?

　　　　(ii)　Why did the boy plan to give the cow the 'greatest hiding of her life' (l. 45)?

　　　　(iii)　List the different feelings the boy has during the incident. Give **examples** from your own life of similar feelings.

　　b　(i)　Neil Gunn sometimes suggests a point rather than telling his reader the details. What is he suggesting by:

　　　　　　(a)　'From gleaned information' (l. 8)

　　　　　　(b)　'revelling in a growth of rare succulence' (ll. 16–17)

　　　　　　(c)　'The time for payment was not yet' (l. 39)

　　　　　　(d)　'something behind that he wasn't supposed to see but saw' (ll. 72–73)

　　　　(ii)　How would you **interpret** the last sentence – 'It spoiled everything?

2　'His elder brother got the whole story out of him' (ll. 78–79).

　　a　In pairs, write the **dialogue** you think the two brothers might have had (do not include the dialogue in lines 82–90).

　　b　Tape-record the dialogue.

　　c　Listen to the dialogue produced by the other pairs, saying what is good or weak about them. Try to list the **criteria** (e.g. Is the speaking clear? Are the boys' characters brought over?) by which you make the judgements.

3　Write a short **appreciation** of this extract, dealing with (a) the author's understanding of the boy; (b) the use of detail; (c) any other interesting features.

4 Cornered

Anne-Louise Verteuil and Nicola Brooks

'The only buttons we wear now,' say the two young authors of *The Teenage Market Place*, 'are marked "Not for Sale"'. Their book is a protest against 'those who make money mercilessly out of the teenage market' and also against the young people who allow themselves to be exploited. Here, Nicola returns home after a trip to the 'wonders of lay-about London'.

When I arrived home my parents, as usual, said little about my trip to London and did not seem really interested in what I'd been doing. I played a lot on my 'cello, took it out on the poor strings – Bach was my favourite. London seemed far away. I made notes, wrote poems. I was very rude to my parents and their guests. Sometimes I threw   5
down my pen while writing when I heard Mummy's footsteps approaching. Why did I do this? But I couldn't find the answer. I used to tire quickly then, and frequently cried secretly, then giggled at something that can't have been amusing.

Again I was mad with my parents when they lectured about having   10
certain standards to live up to. I couldn't understand what standards. Was it the standards of randy lords in the government who slunk off secretly to lay prostitutes and took drugs? Or the Watergate bugging standards? Or were they talking about the standards I read about all the time in the press and saw on television – violence, pornography,   15
cheating? Perhaps it was the standards of a fashionable boarding school with frustrating stripteases in the dormitory, yobs queueing in the lane, and others with their dope, filthy books and magazines for girls that treated sex like a new invention? Or was it the standards of knowing how to lay on a perfect cocktail party, the right apologies,   20
the right amount of snobbery, the false sweetness of a voice on the telephone, the sickening hypocrisy; knowing how to arrive late to show that you were not drooling to come, had visited bigger mansions, more important people; the right tone of voice when you said how pleased you were to see someone you despised?   25

I was desperate, felt cornered – was there only this artificial life and the other one of perverts in Piccadilly, grunting hippies, pot-smoking?

Once more I took refuge in Nature. I went on long lonely walks, roamed the estate, watched the birds, the swans on the lake, felt the   30

11

wind and the rain and the sun on my face. But this was only a tiny part of England, and I couldn't spend all my life sitting on a tractor ploughing fields and watching gulls. When I moved out to a town like Leicester or even to a village, turned on television, glanced at a girls' magazine, saw a newspaper headline, I was in it again. Only those *35* who have lived out of England for any length of time realise how it presses round you, and how insecure are these small islands of peace where it is impossible to live all the time.

One Sunday morning my mother called me a heathen because I hadn't gone to church with the family. She said it laughingly but it *40* hurt. I still couldn't find myself paying homage to a God who was brought out for an hour once a week in a sermon.

I envied men who seemed to have the world at their feet, could go anywhere and do anything, wished I hadn't been born a female. I got so desperate and bored once that I went into Leicester and *45* approached a grotesquely dressed hippy with a guitar strapped to his back. He was a cockney who'd taken a day off manual work to bum around. He could say nothing at all that interested me so I returned to my island of birds and trees and my dreams.

Pausing for a moment, drawing back and trying to look at myself *50* and my behaviour objectively, I wonder why my experiences in London haven't taught me a lesson? I was fifteen, bored, lonely; my only refuge was Nature, books, writing. But I also had a body. Surely, if I was sane, my experiences in London, my observations of teenagers who had simply rotted away thinking they were happy, would have *55* cured me? Some might say I've got a chip on my shoulder, but this is not true – I haven't a grudge against anybody, I'd just like to hit back at those who would injure me while virtually a child without caring, for profit, and these people were all adults.

I hate being told I'm privileged. What exactly does this mean? Does *60* it mean I haven't got to worry about my next meal, was sent to a good school, met rich people, live on a big estate? What has this got to do with the Teenage Marketplace? We teenagers of all classes are reached and degraded by exploiters through discothèques, television, pop festivals, magazines, etc. In fact I've noticed that there are *65* probably more of the so-called privileged ones caught up in the exploiters' net. Could it be that the privileged have a less well-knit family life, due to boarding schools, materialism, superficial society, where no sort of adversity holds one together as a family. It is noticeable how the privileged teenagers of today search for primitive *70* and basic things.

From *The Teenage Market Place*

1 a   (i) Why was Nicola 'mad' with her parents when they lectured her about 'standards' (ll. 10–25)?

      (ii) Why does Nicola feel 'cornered' (l. 26)?

     (iii) Why was Nature not really a refuge for her?

     (iv) How far do you sympathise with her?

      (v) Would you also like to 'hit back' at those who injure young people (ll. 57–58)? If so, how would you do so?

  b The writer's **style** ranges between **formal** expression (e.g. 'teenagers of all classes are reached and degraded by exploiters' (ll. 63–64)) and **informal** (e.g. 'to bum around' (ll. 47–48)). Find other examples of these and decide whether this variety helps the writer's aim or not.

2 An important **theme** in this passage is the exploitation of teenagers.

  a Find out by **research** and enquiry the meaning of the term 'exploitation'.

  b Discuss the question: How far and in what ways are teenagers being exploited today?

3   *Either* **a**   A few lines further in the book Nicola writes:

'If I'd been older and more stable I'm sure I wouldn't have listened to Jane when she suggested a good "scene" in Cornwall. Or is this an excuse for my stupidity?

Anyhow we started planning.

Camping was out – our parents would not allow it. But they agreed that we could take a room. We were free in the big lay-about strip of the West Country. It was more comfortable than camping. Poor parents – do any of them know what's happening?'

Write three or four paragraphs to follow this, imitating Nicola's **style** and reflecting her attitudes.

or **b**   Imagine that time has passed and Nicola herself now has a teenage daughter. Give the daughter's account of her own relationship with her parents.

5 Ah Bumped Ma Heid in the Sheuch
William McIlvanney

Cornelius (or Conn) Docherty is born into a Scottish mining family early this century. This incident at school illustrates one of the problems he faces.

'Docherty!' Less a voice than an effulgence of sound falling across their suddenly stricken silence. Outwith its paralysing glare, others freeze. Conn stands up slowly, carefully doesn't look at anybody else, as if a glance might prove infectious. They all wait. 'Simpson! Would you two creatures come out here.' 5

They are allowed to stand on the floor for a moment, to become the relief of the others, a moral.

'You'll excuse us, Miss Carmichael. I wouldn't want to get blood on your floor.'

Some titters are gratefully offered, withdrawn. Silence is safest. 10

'Certainly, Mr Pirrie.'

They pass into the next room. Their small procession isn't a unique sight but they gain a brief attention here too. Beyond this room, a small cloakroom area, where they stop.

Conn almost swoons with the staleness of the place. It is a small 15 passageway, foetid with forgotten children, a knackery for futures. He sees the drifting motes as clear as constellations. Two coats hang damp. Their quality of sadness haunts his inarticulacy. Mr Pirrie inflates, enormous in the silence, hovers like a Zeppelin.

'Well, well, well. Who started it?' 20

On one of the floorboards an accentuation in the grain makes a road. It runs winding, vanishes under Mr Pirrie's boot.

'It doesn't matter. You'll both be getting the same. What's wrong with your face, Docherty?'

'Skint ma nose, sur.' 25

'How?'

'Ah fell an' bumped ma heid in the sheuch, sur.'

'I beg your pardon?'

'Ah fell an' bumped ma heid in the sheuch, sur.'

'I beg your pardon?' 30

In the pause Conn understands the nature of the choice, tremblingly, compulsively, makes it.

'Ah fell an' bumped ma heid in the sheuch, sur.'

The blow is instant. His ear seems to enlarge, is muffed in

numbness. But it's only the dread of tears that hurts. Mr Pirrie   *35*
distends on a lozenge of light which mustn't be allowed to break. It
doesn't. Conn hasn't cried.

'That, Docherty, is impertinence. You will translate, please, into
the mother-tongue.'

The blow is a mistake, Conn knows. If he tells his father, he will   *40*
come up to the school. 'Ye'll take whit ye get wi' the strap an' like it.
But if anybody takes their hauns tae ye, ye'll let me ken.' He thinks
about it. But the problem is his own. It frightens him more to imagine
his father coming up.

'I'm waiting, Docherty. What happened?'   *45*

'I bumped my head, sir.'

'Where? Where did you bump it, Docherty?'

'In the gutter, sir.'

'Not an inappropriate setting for you, if I may say so.'

The words mean nothing. Only what happens counts.   *50*

'I'm disappointed in you, Docherty. You'll soon be coming up to
the big school. And I'll be ready for you. I used to hear nice things
about you. But not any more. You might've had the chance to go to
the Academy. You still could. Do you know what that means? But
what's the point? I wouldn't waste the time of highly qualified men.   *55*
But while you're here you'll behave like civilised people. Brawling in
the playground!'

His voice shudders the wood around them. The words have
worked, mystically invoke his anger. It possesses him. The veins in his
nose suffuse. The strap snakes out from its nest under the shoulder of   *60*
his jacket.

'Simpson first!' It is a ritual. He holds the strap in his right hand,
drops it over his shoulder, reaches back with his left hand, flexes the
leather, begins. 'I will *not*. Have. Violence. In my school.'

Four. Conn can prepare.   *65*

'Docherty!' One. Conn recites to himself: *Ah bumped ma heid in the
sheuch*. Two. *Sheuch*. 'You're getting as bad as your brother was.'
Three. *Fat man*. 'I was glad to get rid of him.' Four. Conn's hands
drop, stiff as plaster-casts. 'Up, Docherty, up! Two more for
insolence.' Five. *Bastard*. He is watching for signs of tears. Six. *Big,*   *70*
fat bastard.

He has become his hands. His will huddles round them, containing
the radiations of their pain, refusing them the salve of tears. The two
of them are led back to the room.

Mr Pirrie says, 'I've just been tickling these two's hands. As a little   *75*
warning. The next boys I catch behaving like savages won't be able to
use their hands for a week.'

[Miss Carmichael continues the lesson, pondering on the punishment the two boys
have received. Simpson is crying, while Conn thinks about the conflict between his
home and school life.]

While Miss Carmichael gave him sympathetic exemption from her questions, he took a stub of pencil in his fingers. Slowly across a scuffed piece of paper a word moved clumsily. Opposite it another *80* word was manoeuvred and settled, the way he had seen in a dictionary Miss Carmichael showed him. His hand shook as he did it. It was a painful and tremulous matter, like an ant trying to manipulate stones. He sat buried inside himself while the words spread themselves across the paper. Minutes later, he was stunned into stillness, looking at the *85* big awkward shapes they made before him.

sheuch	*gutter*	
speugh	*sparrow*	
lum	*chimny*	
brace	*mantalpiece*	*90*
bine	*tub*	
coom	*soot*	
coomie	*foolish man (Mr Pirrie)*	
gomeril	*another foolish man*	
spicket	*tap*	*95*
glaur	*muck what is in a puddle after the puddle goes away*	
wabbit	*tired*	
whaup	*curloo*	
tumshie	*turnip*	*100*
breeks	*troosers*	
chanty	*po*	
preuch	*anything you can get*	
I was taigled longer nor	*I was kept back for a more longer*	
I ettled	*time than I desired.*	*105*

One side of the paper was filled. He didn't start on the other side because he now wanted to write things that he couldn't find any English for. When something sad had happened and his mother was meaning that there wasn't anything you could do about it, she would say 'ye maun dree yer weird'. When she was busy, she had said she was *110* 'saund-papered tae a whuppet.' 'Pit a raker oan the fire.' 'Handcuffed to Mackindoe's ghost.' 'A face tae follow a flittin'.' If his father had to give him a row but wasn't really angry, he said 'Ah'll skelp yer bum wi' a tealeaf tae yer nose bluids.'

Conn despaired of English. Suddenly, with the desperation of a *115* man trying to amputate his own infected arm, he savagely scored out all the English equivalents.

On his way out of school, he folded his grubby piece of paper very carefully and put it in his pocket. It was religiously preserved for weeks. By the time he lost it, he didn't need it. *120*

From *Docherty*

1 a (i) Why is Conn being punished?
     (ii) If you had been the schoolmaster, what would you have done?
     (iii) What is Conn's father's attitude to punishment at school? Do you agree with it?
     (iv) 'You will translate, please, into the mother-tongue' (ll. 38–39). Why is this remark important for understanding the whole extract?
     (v) Why does Conn savagely score out 'the English equivalents' (l. 117)?

  b The author, William McIlvanney, takes care to reveal:
     (i) Conn's physical sensations; (ii) his feelings; (iii) his thoughts. Find **examples** of each of these.

2 *Either* **a** Practise and record a dramatised reading of the extract. Include a **narrator,** the pupils and the teachers taking part in the action (you will need to write some lines for Miss Carmichael) and appropriate sound effects.
    Or **b** In groups discuss the **proposition** that **dialect** speaking should be discouraged in the classroom. Check first, by enquiry or **research**, the meaning of '**dialect**' and the difference between it and '**accent**'.

3 a Outline the possible stages for a project on *Dialect*.
     (i) Begin by listing words and phrases from your local dialect.
     (ii) Consider ways of putting these into groups.
     (iii) Suggest how you would gather a wider range of samples of dialect, from different areas.
     (iv) Write some questions, which your **survey** would help you to answer, about the use of dialect, both present and future.

  b Describe the possible course of Conn's life over the next few years.

6 No Matter How Perfect
We Think We Are,
We Are All Handicapped
In One Way or Another
Norman Britton

The candle flickered ominously in the wind and at any moment the flame would go out. In many ways my life was like that, only it was not the wind that threatened my existence but people and their attitudes. There is nothing more humiliating than a person being treated like an idiot or worse. 5

For most of my life I bore the brunt of other people's ignorance and lived a life of comparative seclusion. I was born with a speech impediment and as I became older my lower jaw grew out of proportion to the rest of my face. My days at school were black and awesome, and consisted mainly of cruel taunts from the other 10 children. There were also times of happiness, but they were the exception rather than the rule. The older I became the more selfish I grew and I was constantly thinking about myself. This meant that I had very little interest in anyone outside of my own family.

When I left school I obtained employment in a supermarket. For 15 the first time in my life I had been accepted in an environment, outside my family, that wasn't hostile.

There was still the outside world to contend with, as people still continued to laugh at me on the street. I found solace in alcohol and for a while it was a means by which I could forget the pain other 20 people inflicted upon me because of their inability to understand. There were also times when I contemplated suicide. But somehow the easy way out wasn't quite so easy. So there I was, just 20 years old, with my whole life ahead of me. But I couldn't talk clearly, I looked odd and people frequently laughed at me. How was I going to survive 25 in a world that seemed to be against me?

I had tried for many years to obtain some kind of surgery to improve my facial appearance, but was always told there was no such surgery available. But I persisted, and eventually found myself at the Eastman Dental Hospital, where I was told about corrective surgery 30 that could be carried out if I was willing to undergo a period of orthodontic treatment beforehand. I agreed and four months later the treatment began. It was another 18 months before my teeth were ready for the jaw operation.

In November 1980 I entered the Royal National Ear, Nose and *35*
Throat Hospital in London and had surgery on my lower jaw. The
operation was performed by a team led by Professor M. Harris and
lasted some six hours. It also proved to be of sufficient interest for
BBC's *Nationwide* to make a documentary programme about my life
and subsequent operation. This was transmitted in 1981. At the same *40*
time I was introduced to the local Baptist Church. At first I was
resentful, and felt that if there was a God he had done me a bad turn in
making me the way he did. But over a period of 18 months I
eventually became a Christian. In the church to which I now belong I
was shaken by the love and compassion that the people showed me, *45*
and it was this that led me to find out more about Christianity.

My operation was successful, and with the love and support of
friends and family I was soon on the road to a full recovery. It was a
difficult time: I was on liquid food for eight weeks, a metal frame was
fastened to my face and my jaws were locked together by two metal *50*
splints. I am still a prisoner of myself, for the past lingers menacingly
as I struggle to live with my new face. It is not easy to live in a world
where people constantly reject you, and then suddenly to be thrust
into a world of complete acceptance, simply because of an operation.
I still struggle with myself and lack of confidence but I am now able to *55*
do the things which were once were beyond me.

One of the most important things I have learnt in the last year is
that we are all handicapped in some way or other, and that no matter
how perfect we think we are there is something about each of us that
makes us different from everyone else. My hope for the future is that *60*
people will accept the disabled as *people* because that's what they are.
Society needs to recognise the wants and needs of everyone and not
just those who are considered normal. In today's world we all need to
feel that we, disabled people as well, are acceptable and able to fulfil
our personal lives and make a meaningful contribution to everyday *65*
life, however limited that may be.

From *The Times*, 29 September 1982

1 **a** (i) Do you agree with the title? Say why or why not.
   (ii) What in your view were Norman Britton's two worst
        problems? How did he solve them?
   (iii) Describe two or three difficulties which the BBC Nationwide
        team must have had in making their documentary
        programme.
  b (i) The writer leaves the reader to imagine various details to fill
        out what he says in the article. How would you do this for:

        (a) 'I found solace in alcohol' (l. 19); (b) 'the easy way out wasn't so easy' (ll. 22–23); (c) 'I am now able to do the things which were once beyond me' (ll. 55–56)?

  (ii) Some of the writer's opinions could be labelled **opinion**, others **fact**.

        (a) What is the difference between the two?

        (b) Find two **examples** of each in the article.

2   Anthony Armstrong, MP, having read this article, feels that life could be better for many disabled people.

  a In small groups, act out the interviews he might have with three such people in his constituency.

  b Tape-record part of the speech he might make on the same **topic** in Parliament.

3   Using your imagination or experience, write a few paragraphs from a **biography** or **autobiography** which illustrate some of the ideas in the last paragraph of the passage. You will find an example of biography in *The Cow*, pages 1–12, and of autobiography in *Cornered*, pages 13–14.

7 Black Like Me
J. H. Griffin

Some years ago, at a time when racial questions were the cause of controversy and conflict in the USA, a white man decided to undergo medical treatment to turn himself black. Then he travelled widely in the USA, recording his impressions.

My money was running low so I decided to cash some traveller's cheques before leaving. The banks were closed, since it was past noon on Saturday, but I felt I would have no difficulty with traveller's cheques in any of the larger stores, especially those on Dryades where I had traded and was known as a customer.   *5*

I took the bus to Dryades and walked down it, stopping at the dime store where I'd made most of my purchases. The young white girl came forward to wait on me.

'I need to cash a traveller's cheque,' I said smiling.

'We don't cash any cheques of any kind,' she said firmly.   *10*

'But a traveller's cheque is perfectly safe,' I said.

'We just don't cash cheques,' she said and turned away.

'Look, you know me. You've waited on me. I need some money.'

'You should have gone to the bank.'

'I didn't know I needed money until after the banks closed,' I said.   *15*

I knew I was making a pest of myself but I could scarcely believe this nice young lady could be so unsympathetic, so insolent when she discovered I did not come in to buy something.

'I'll be glad to buy a few things,' I said.

She called up to the book-keeping department on an open   *20*
mezzanine. 'Hey! Do we cash traveller's ch—'

'No!' the white woman shouted back.

'Thank you for your kindness,' I said and walked out.

I went into one store after the other along Dryades and Rampart Streets. In every store their smiles turned to grimaces when they saw I   *25*
meant not to buy but to cash a cheque. It was not their refusal – I could understand that; it was the bad manners they displayed. I began to feel desperate and resentful. They would have cashed a traveller's cheque without hesitation for a white man. Each time they refused me, they implied clearly that I had probably come by these cheques   *30*
dishonestly and they wanted nothing to do with them or me.

Finally, after I gave up hope and decided I must remain in New Orleans without funds until the banks opened on Monday, I walked towards town. Small gold lettering on the window of a store caught

my attention: CATHOLIC BOOK STORE. Knowing the Catholic stand on *35*
racism, I wondered if this shop might cash a Negro's cheque. With
some hesitation, I opened the door and entered. I was prepared to be
disappointed.

'Would you cash a twenty-dollar traveller's cheque for me?' I asked
the proprietress. *40*

'Of course,' she said without hesitation, as though nothing could be
more natural. She did not even study me.

I was so grateful I bought a number of paper-back books – works
of Maritain, Aquinas and Christopher Dawson. With these in my
jacket, I hurried towards the Greyhound bus station. *45*

In the bus station lobby, I looked for signs indicating a coloured
waiting-room, but saw none. I walked up to the ticket counter. When
the lady ticket-seller saw me, her otherwise attractive face turned
sour, violently so. This look was so unexpected and so unprovoked I
was taken aback. *50*

'What do you want?' she snapped.

Taking care to pitch my voice to politeness, I asked about the next
bus to Hattiesburg.

She answered rudely and glared at me with such loathing I knew I
was receiving what the Negroes call 'the hate stare'. It was my first *55*
experience with it. It is far more than the look of disapproval one
occasionally gets. This was so exaggeratedly hateful I would have
been amused if I had not been so surprised.

I framed the words in my mind: 'Pardon me, but have I done
something to offend you?' But I realized I had done nothing – my *60*
colour offended her.

'I'd like a one-way ticket to Hattiesburg, please,' I said and placed a
ten-dollar bill on the counter.

'I can't change that big bill,' she said abruptly and turned away, as
though the matter were closed. I remained at the window, feeling *65*
strangely abandoned but not knowing what else to do. In a while she
flew back at me, her face flushed, and fairly shouted: 'I *told* you – I
can't change that big bill.'

'Surely,' I said stiffly, 'in the entire Greyhound system there must be
some means of changing a ten-dollar bill. Perhaps the manager—' *70*

She jerked the bill furiously from my hand and stepped away from
the window. In a moment she reappeared to hurl my change and the
ticket on the counter with such force most of it fell on the floor at my
feet. I was truly dumbfounded by this deep fury that possessed her
whenever she looked at me. Her performance was so venomous, I felt *75*
sorry for her. It must have shown in my expression, for her face
congested to high pink. She undoubtedly considered it a supreme
insolence for a Negro to dare to feel sorry for her.

I stooped to pick up my change and ticket from the floor. I
wondered how she would feel if she learned that the Negro before *80*

whom she had behaved in such an unlady-like manner was habitually a white man.

With almost an hour before bus departure, I turned away and looked for a place to sit. The large, handsome room was almost empty. No other Negro was there, and I dared not take a seat unless I *85* saw some other Negro also seated.

Once again a 'hate stare' drew my attention like a magnet. It came from a middle-aged, heavy-set, well-dressed white man. He sat a few yards away fixing his eyes on me. Nothing can describe the withering horror of this. You feel lost, sick at heart before such unmasked *90* hatred, not so much because it threatens you as because it shows humans in such an inhuman light. You see a kind of insanity, something so obscene the very obscenity of it (rather than its threat) terrifies you. It was so new I could not take my eyes from the man's face. I felt like saying: 'What in God's name are you doing to *95* yourself?'

A Negro porter sidled over to me. I glimpsed his white coat and turned to him. His glance met mine and communicated the sorrow, the understanding.

'Where am I supposed to go?' I asked him. *100*

He touched my arm in that mute and reassuring way of men who share a moment of crisis. 'Go outside and around the corner of the building. You'll find the room.'

The white man continued to stare, his mouth twisted with loathing as he turned his head to watch me move away. *105*

In the coloured waiting-room, which was not labelled as such, but rather as COLOURED CAFÉ, presumably because of inter-state travel regulations, I took the last empty seat. The room was crowded with glum faces, faces dead to all enthusiasm, faces of people waiting.

The books I had bought from the Catholic Book Store weighed *110* heavily in my pocket. I pulled one of them out and, without looking at the title, let it fall open in my lap. I read:

'. . . *it is by justice that we can authentically measure man's value or his nullity . . . the absence of justice is the absence of what makes him man.*' Plato. *115*

I have heard it said another way, as a dictum: '*He who is less than just is less than man.*'

I copied the passage in a little pocket note-book. A Negro woman, her face expressionless, flat, high-lighted with sweat, watched me write. When I turned in my seat to put the note-book in my hip *120* pocket, I detected the faintest smile at the corners of her mouth.

From *Black Like Me*

23

Lionel and Mary Jackson

1 **a** Say
   (i) why the dime-store assistant will not, and
   (ii) why the proprietress of the Catholic book store *will* cash a traveller's cheque for the author (ll. 6–23 and 34–45).
   (iii) Why does the author feel so 'sick at heart' when he experiences 'the hate stare' (ll. 54–58 and 87–96)?
   (iv) Why do you think the Negro woman is smiling faintly (ll. 118–121)?
   (v) What response do you think the writer hopes the reader will make to this passage?

  b **Descriptions** of people are an important part of this passage. Make a list of the people described and say why the author includes each one.

2 Discuss these questions:
  a Is J H Griffin cheating by disguising himself as a Negro?
  b What do we mean by 'racial prejudice'?
  c How should we interpret 'He who is less than just is less than man' (ll. 116–117)?

3 Re-read the extract, paying attention to (a) the author's attitudes and (b) the use of detail. Then imagine a further incident in his life and describe it in a similar **autobiographical** form.

8 Sexploitation
Zoe Bell

It is agreed by most intelligent people that women have been exploited by men for far too long and that it is high time women had a fairer share of the opportunities in life.

Women are fed-up with being second-class citizens prized only for their 'looks', their 'cooking' and their 'obedience to men'! 5

Just take a look at these priceless snippets which appeared in print recently. Do they show women in good light? Do they give a picture of a society which is being fair and open-minded to girls?

'A family treats itself to a video so that the junior members can keep a visual record of the Cup Final, so that Dad won't miss the final 10 episodes of his favourite comedy programme because of the darts match, and so that Mum can see Des O'Connor over and over again while she's doing the ironing in the morning!' – *Shropshire Star.*

'I think cooking is a subject for boys and girls, because if boys don't get married they will have to cook for themselves.' – Unnamed boy 15 on *A Question of Equality*, BBC2.

'Women whose husbands won't normally let them go out at night are happy to do so if the destination is a slimming club.' – *Northwich Guardian.*

'London's girl chess prodigy, Sabrena Needham, nine, of Queen's 20 Park Junior School, triumphed over the brainiest boys last night for the third year running. We never expected a result like Sabrena's. It looks as if we shan't be able to give her the top trophy as it is designed for boys.' – *The New Standard.*

'So let us not forget. God commanded a man to rule properly over his 25 wife. (Gen. 3:16). Women these days are increasingly ruling over weak and ineffectual men contrary to God's law. God will punish both men and women for forsaking their proper roles (verses 16–18).' – *Plain Truth.*

'A Swiss Company has developed a can that heats the food inside 30 automatically. Obviously it will be a boon to outdoor enthusiasts, the armed forces, rescue teams, people who want a hot meal at their desks or workbenches – and lazy housewives.' – *Daily Mail.*

From *Payday*

Lionel and Mary Jackson

1 a   (i) Explain the title of the extract.
      (ii) This article could be described as 'anti-sexist'. By reading and questioning, decide what this means.
      (iii) (a) What **evidence** could be given to support the opening statement of the article; (b) Would you describe the statement as **fact** or **opinion**?
      (iv) What is meant by 'priceless' (l. 6); 'open-minded' (l. 8)?

   b   (i) Invent two other 'snippets' which Zoe Bell might have used in her article.
      (ii) Which of the following **inferences** (i) can (ii) cannot be drawn from the passage:
      (a) Women do not like being admired for their looks.
      (b) Society at present is not fair to girls.
      (c) Some people think that women should be ruled by men.
      (d) The author agrees with these people (above).
      (e) Boys do not like cooking.

2   Write and tape-record a speech which you think Zoe Bell would like to hear made against 'sexploitation'. Mention the occasion, the audience and the purpose for the speech.

3   Under the headings *Speech and Action* and *Vision* write part of a television play involving an argument over sex-roles, which are the patterns males and females are generally expected to follow in society.

9 'These Kids Today'
Carrie Carmichael

Every child is color coded at birth. Its name is typed on a pink-for-girl, blue-for-boy card that is placed at the head of the hospital bassinet. It is wrapped in a pink or blue blanket in the nursery lest an observer forget it is a girl or a boy, and mistake it for a baby.

All babies are born the same color – a blue-gray translucence. Only   *5*
with the first breath does each baby change from blue-gray to black or white or brown or yellow. All children come out equal, but quickly race is noted, sex is checked, and the world begins the process of imprinting on that baby what it wants from a brown girl, a black boy, a white girl, a yellow boy. The expectations vary for each race, sex,   *10*
and social class.

"The little boy screams leaving his mother's womb and in the delivery room they say, 'He's all boy,'" observed Dr. Robert E. Gould. "The girl screams and yells and they ignore it till she smiles and then they say, 'Isn't she pretty? She'll be a heart-breaker when she   *15*
grows up.' Early on they learn what is approved, what is not approved. It starts from day one. A little boy is born, you throw it up in the air, catch it. Nobody would throw a little girl baby, she's too fragile. What a difference in the way you handle the babies at the age of one day. Long before they understand the language, they   *20*
understand the non-verbal communication."

One active feminist experimented with her newborn. As she wheeled the baby in the carriage she would tell some passersby that the baby was a boy. "My, he looks strong," they would remark and take a swipe at "his" arm. When she said that the baby was a girl,   *25*
"she" would be patted, stroked, and told "she" was pretty. The mother had proof positive, right in her own neighborhood, of how differently boys and girls are treated. One day the baby could tolerate swipes, another day the same baby could only endure a soft pat. Strength and sex-role behavior are only in the eye of the beholder.   *30*

A baby's sex is all important. Few hospitals are radical enough to wrap all babies in yellow or type BABY CARMICHAEL on the identifying card. In 1977 we are still stuck in the girl/boy rut. The first question anyone asks after a birth is, "What is it?" The questioner is asking the sex with an assumption that when the sex of a child is known a great   *35*
deal about that child has been revealed.

Lois Gould wrote a fanciful story about a child whose sex was hidden from all except itself and its parents. *X: A Fabulous Child's Story* tells the tale of a special experiment to raise an X, a child, not a boy or a girl. Adults in the story were confounded and embarrassed   *40*

27

Lionel and Mary Jackson

by an X. They knew the appropriate toys and clothing to give girls and boys, but what did you give an X? Even X's schoolmates were at first disturbed and later radicalized by X's freedom to basket weave and shoot baskets, to race and bake.

From *Non-sexist Childraising*

1 a (i) Does the writer think that babies should or should not be 'colour-coded' (l. 1)?
   (ii) By 'sex-role behavior' (l. 27, US spelling) we mean acting in the way society expects girls and women or boys and men to behave. Recall some incidents from your own life when you were happy or unhappy with your sex-role.
   (iii) What do we mean by 'feminist' (l. 20)? Why is there no recognised word 'masculist'?
   (iv) Why were the adults in Lois Gould's story 'embarrassed by an X' (l. 37)?
   (v) Outline the rest of Lois Gould's story as you would imagine it.
2 Here is the beginning of a children's story called *Lucy* by Catherine Storr (Bodley Head, 1961)

Lucy wanted to be a boy.

She was the youngest of three sisters. Jane and Caroline had never wanted to be anything but what they were. They contentedly wore skirts and petticoats: they played at dolls' tea parties and Mothers and Fathers. They learnt dancing and did not object to being told they looked pretty. But Lucy did.

She didn't want to wear dresses. She didn't like dolls. When Caroline offered to help her play at houses, Lucy only wanted to use the house as a Red Indian wigwam and to scalp Caroline, who had long curly hair. She never opened the box that held the dolls' tea set with a pink rose at the bottom of each cup. In a corner of Jane's and Caroline's bedroom stood the dolls' house, for which they were now really too old, getting dustier and dustier. Inside, Mr and Mrs Fifty-three lay sadly on the drawing-room floor, while grandfather sat for ever at the piano composing an endless lament for the forgetfulness of young girls.

Lucy collected weapons. She had a drawer full of guns: she had a popgun which shot out a cork, a pistol which shot caps, a pistol which didn't shoot caps but should have and a shot gun. She had a short dagger and a long sword and a very long thin thing rather like a sword, with a sort of button at the end, which was called a foil.

Upstairs in her bedroom she had a cowboy suit, an outfit of plastic armour, complete with shield and helmet, and a clown's suit that had belonged to Caroline. The frocks the other two girls had worn were pushed away to the back of her chest of drawers and covered up by the slacks and jeans and shorts that Lucy liked to wear.

She tried to persuade her mother to cut her hair as short as a boy's, but her mother would not agree. Sometimes Lucy threatened to cut it off herself, but although she had once taken the kitchen scissors and snipped a little, she never quite dared to chop off the whole lot.

In groups, decide

a   the age at which a child might appreciate the story;
b   what Lucy does (later in the story) to win the respect of some boys;
c   whether it is fair to describe the story as 'sexist'. You will need to be sure of the meaning of this word before this part of the discussion.

3   Continue *either* **a** this **dialogue**:

Peter: I'm not having him playing with dolls. Never!
Jennifer: But he loves dolls. He's quite a gentle boy really.
Peter: A boy of eight playing with dolls? You don't see young Billy Archer doing that!

Or **b** this one:

Interviewer: Let's get this point quite clear, Dr Block. You're saying that males are temperamentally different from females?
Dr Block: In some respects, yes. Males tend to be more interested in mechanical things, and females in other people.
Interviewer: But surely, this is just because society has conditioned, er, moulded boys and girls in these directions?

10 Family Sell Furniture to Help Tribes

The Times Ipswich Correspondent

Charity began at home yesterday for a widow and her four children after they saw most of their furniture and possessions sold to help starving tribes in Africa.

Mrs Joan Kerr, aged 45, of Frogs Hall Road, Lindsey, Suffolk, decided to sell her household "luxuries" after watching a harrowing *5*
Television film about the famine in Ethiopia.

She said yesterday: "I suddenly realized that we did not need all these things and they could be used to bring life and hope to people in real need."

At a public auction in Lindsey village hall on Saturday 135 lots *10*
from Mrs Kerr's home were sold for more than £3,000, which she is giving to Oxfam's Ethiopia appeal.

The dining room table, chairs and a dish washer, as well as pictures, mirrors and bedside lamps went under the hammer. The highest bid was £355 for the dining room suite and the smallest was £1 for a stone *15*
ginger beer bottle that Mrs Kerr dug up in her garden.

"All we have left is our beds, a few personal things, an old cooker and fridge, and my washing machine. I felt a bit guilty keeping that, but with four children I could not face the thought of doing without it," she said. *20*

Her children all contributed to the sale; Timothy, aged 19, handed over his motor cycle and crash helmet and Emily, aged 14, her youngest daughter, parted with her favourite horse pictures and toys.

Mrs Kerr plans to refurnish her luxury modern home with second-hand goods from junk shops. She added: "I hope our gesture will *25*
make other people stop and think about the plight of the starving".

From *The Times*, 30 May 1983

---

1 a (i) What does the **proverb** 'Charity begins at home' usually mean?
    (ii) What are 'household "luxuries"' (l. 5)?
    (iii) Which items in your home would your family be prepared to sell for charity?
    (iv) Why did Mrs Kerr feel guilty at keeping her washing machine?

(v) What did Mrs Kerr mean by 'our gesture' (l. 25)?

(vi) Do you think Mrs Kerr's action was worthwhile and successful?

b A newspaper 'story' must catch and hold the reader's attention. How does this story try to do this?

2 a Record an imaginary radio **interview** with Mrs Kerr.

b By reading and **research** obtain some facts about inequality between the richer and poorer nations. Then discuss what could or should be done about it.

3 Design (a) the poster which might have advertised the auction sale mentioned in the passage; and (b) a poster advertising another unusual way of raising money for charity.

11 Explosion
Roger Bush

Statistics baffle me, Lord.
Like . . .
Today one hundred and ninety thousand more
of your children sat to break their fast
than did yesterday. 5
Tomorrow,
one hundred and ninety thousand more.
And tomorrow
and tomorrow and tomorrow and tomorrow
Ad infinitum. 10
Today we didn't produce calories enough to
"Give us this day our daily bread".
Some went to bed with empty bellies.
Two thirds of this world's population, people, Lord.
Women, Children, Men. 15
Let's see, Lord, how did I fare today.
Breakfast? Well, bacon, eggs, cereal, milk and sugar,
coffee, toast and marmalade.
For Lunch:
Just a ham salad, some chocolate ice cream 20
and a cuppa.
Dinner I really enjoyed, Lord.
Roast duck, green peas, new potatoes, and
apple pie and cream for sweets. A nice Chablis
and a brandy made the day. 25
Did I forget the morning cup of tea, or
the afternoon spell as well?
and the TV snack ere bed.
O yes, Lord,
two teaspoons full of carb soda. 30
Five loaves and two fishes, Lord.
and five thousand folk.
"For what we are about to receive, Lord,
we are truly thankful".
And for the one hundred and ninety thousand 35
extra for breakfast,
Tomorrow?
Guests?
Amen.

From *Prayers for Pagans*

1 **a** (i) What does the title mean?

(ii) Why does the author call this piece a 'prayer'?

(iii) Why does the writer say 'your' children (l. 4)?

(iv) How did *you* fare yesterday? (see lines 16–30)

(v) Why is 'carb soda' mentioned (l. 30)?

(vi) What is the point of the two sentences in quotation marks (ll. 12 and 33–34)?

b (i) 'Is the writer's purpose the same as or different from that of the writer of *Family Sell Furniture to Help Tribes* (No. 10, p. 35)?

(ii) Which of the two pieces (Nos. 10 and 11) makes you feel more sympathy for the poorer people in the world?

2 Here are some ideas for helping the poorer nations. In your groups decide how you would place them in order of likely usefulness:

(a) Double the tax on pop records and send the money to the poor countries

(b) Help developing countries understand and use contraception

(c) Abolish all nuclear weapons and use the money saved to feed the starving people

(d) Encourage emigration between all countries

(e) Launch a big United Nations scheme to help poorer countries develop their own resources

(f) Finance research into artificial food production

(g) Make meat-eating illegal in the richer countries.

3 Write a 'prayer' in the style of Roger Bush on down-and-outs *or* murderers *or* glue-sniffers *or* suicides *or* a **theme** of your own choice.

33.

12 Smoking
Sue Armstrong

SOME SMOKERS SPEAK

JOE is 24. He gets through about 20 cigarettes a day, though he used to smoke a lot more. He gave up for four months once, and found it hell. He was jittery, on edge and bad tempered, so he started again. This is his story:

"I started smoking at school at the age of 12. I did it because at that 5
age I wanted to look big, and more grown up. I wanted to impress the girls too. Also it was against the rules, and that made a big difference. We were told by our teachers that anyone caught with a packet of cigarettes would be expelled, so it was an exciting thing to do. I think if the teacher had said 'OK, let's all have a smoke', we would have said 10
'no way'.

"The first time I smoked I threw up all over the place, but I had another one because I thought it looked good standing on the corner of the street. The trouble is that when you're very young your biggest ambition is to be older and to be able to say that you are going down 15
the pub with friends, having a drink and a smoke. At that age statistics don't mean a thing. It's all image. By the age of 16 I realised I couldn't give up. Before that it had never crossed my mind that I was 'a smoker', and that I probably would be all my life. I certainly didn't want to be, but you get hooked. The thing is a lot of people who don't 20
smoke tell you there's no pleasure in it. I say nonsense. Smoking definitely feels good, and it's very relaxing. But you don't start smoking because you need to feel relaxed. You start to look good. Then you get dependent on what it does for you, and you can't give it up." 25

MARGARET is now 17, and she has been smoking since she was 13. She and a friend used to hide from their parents on the stairs outside their flats smoking. Margaret says "My mum and dad smoke, and I just thought it's what adults do. I started smoking to look grown up. I used to save lemonade bottles and things to get enough money 30
for fags. Then I got caught by my mum and she was furious. That put me off for a while, but then all my friends in school were smoking – hiding in the toilets and passing the cigarettes along the line, and I took it up again.

"My mum and dad hate me smoking though they smoke a lot 35
themselves. It's probably because they've got to the stage of knowing

what it does to you. I wouldn't like to see a picture of my lungs now, but I can't see them so I'm not really bothered, though I do get a bad cough every winter. I get fed up with smoking when I've got no money left for other things, but I've got no will power and I don't think I *40* could stop now."

EILEEN's story is a bit different. She is now 16 and she too started smoking at 13. But she has never really liked it. "I got in with a crowd and they were all smoking. I couldn't be the only one left out. And at discos and things you can't sit with a bar of chocolate in your hand. *45* For me it's the action, not the cigarette. I don't enjoy smoking—it makes me sick, and I know inside it's a horrible habit. But when all your friends are smoking, it's hard to resist the pressure."

Eileen found it difficult to resist the pressure, but there are lots of people who don't smoke. Some have never felt tempted to try. Some *50* have tried and felt too bad to try it again. And some have very positive reasons for not smoking. . . .

SOME NON-SMOKERS SPEAK

LINSEY MACDONALD is 17. About 6 years ago she took up running seriously, and when she was only 16 she won a bronze medal at the Olympic games in Moscow. She broke the British 400 metre *55* record, and recently she broke the British record for the 600 metres as well. Linsey says:

"I have never smoked because I was always interested in sports. You have to be at your peak of health if you want to be any good in sport, and you can never reach that peak if you smoke. I've never been *60* under any pressure to try it. Some of my friends at school do smoke, but I think they're the odd ones out. I think it could be classed as old-fashioned nowadays. It's not necessarily the done thing any more. That's my experience anyway."

JANE is now 26, and she has never been a smoker. "It sounds *65* strange, but I don't smoke for the very reason people do start smoking. When I was younger at parties and things I thought people who were just starting looked silly puffing smoke in and out quickly, not knowing how to hold a cigarette and a glass at the same time, and getting smoke in their faces so that their eyes watered. I knew I'd *70* probably be the same, and I didn't want to make a fool of myself. Then you get past the stage where everyone is experimenting and people don't pressurise you any more anyway. The main advantage of not smoking is that when you go out with friends it makes you feel good to be the one who isn't skint. You can usually pay your way *75* when others are often hanging around wondering whether anyone will pay for them."

From *Smoking: What's in it for you?*

1 **a**   (i) Which speaker in the passage might have each of these **points of view**:
(a) 'Physical fitness is vital if I'm to fulfil my ambitions'
(b) 'Smoking gives you a sort of status'
(c) 'When you are one of a group you do what the others do'
(d) 'Smoking is quite enjoyable, and soothing'
(e) 'It's really a waste of money – smoking'
(f) 'It's not good to smoke, but people need something to do when they get together'
(g) 'Why should they tell me not to smoke when they do it themselves?'
(h) 'Smoking doesn't have the appeal it had once'
(i) 'If they could see how pathetic they looked, they wouldn't do it'
(j) 'I agree it's a waste of money but some people, like me, just can't break the habit!'
(ii) Should smoking be banned in cinemas, on public transport, in hospitals, cafes, discos, or altogether?
(iii) Can you fill in the blanks to complete these points against smoking which the author gives later in the book:
(a) No-one particularly likes the smell of smoke on their ____' in their ____ or on their ____ (and even less on someone else's)
(b) nor smoke from someone else's ____ end drifting into their ____
(c) nor the stale ____ of a room after a ____
(d) nor the ____ in their mouths after a ____ smoking session
(e) nor the sight of a full ____
(f) nor the ____ of a heavy smoker clearing his ____ and ____
(g) and no one would ____ choose to dull their senses of ____ and ____, nor make it difficult for themselves to run and catch a ____.

   b   What might be revealed by the 'statistics' referred to by Joe (l. 16) and the 'picture of my lungs' mentioned by Margaret (l. 37)?

2   Find out (a) how many people in your class smoke; (b) whether they are in the majority or the minority; (c) the reasons usually

given for smoking (d) whether your class group is typical of the population as a whole (you will need to do some **research** for this).

3   Write a humorous piece on either:

a   'Smoking in the Twentieth Century' by a writer living in the Twenty-third Century.

or **b**   'My First Cigarette' by a space alien.

13 After You, Robinson Crusoe
Macdonald Hastings

'People are forever writing "let's pretend" stories about desert island adventures,' says Macdonald Hastings at the beginning of his book. 'I am the only person alive who, out of my own experience, can give you some practical answers. On 6 August, 1960, three hundred and one years after Robinson Crusoe, I was cast away on the desert island of Resourse . . . Unlike Robinson Crusoe, I did it on purpose. I wanted to learn whether I could look after myself, without benefit of as much as a ship's biscuit (never mind a comb and toothbrush) for five weeks.'

Fifteenth Day: Two more notches to add to the score so far: the fifteenth notch in the trunk of the coconut tree on which I am keeping count of the days that I am on the island. Another notch in my belt.

When I landed I had three holes to spare beyond the buckle. To tighten my belt now I have had to pierce the leather an inch behind the 5 last of them. I'm that much thinner. But I believe that I am that much fitter too. My middle-aged pot has vanished. I've got rid of my early morning smoker's cough. At last, that wretched disc-jockey in my head is off the air. My hand is so steady that I know that I am holding the Leicas at tenth-of-a-second exposures like a rock, something I 10 haven't been able to achieve for years.

Of course, I'm existing on what's called an unbalanced diet. All protein, very little greenstuff. I'm burning energy at the rate of eighty-four hours a week of hard manual labour after coming straight from an office desk. But now that I have a roof over my head, life ought to 15 be easier. I shall have more time to think about food.

The agronomist at Mahé was convinced that a man can live for a limited period on coconuts alone. The doctor insisted that I must fell the palms to get what's called 'the millionaire's salad'. The salad is the growing heart of the tree. It eats very like celery. But, just as I am 20 reluctant to kill animals for the hell of it, so also I would like to think that I can pull through without laying more trees than I have to. On my present diet, limited though it is, I ought to be all right. Eating the same things as I am myself, there's nothing much wrong with Friday.*

I'm in no doubt that, in civilized life, we all eat too much. In 25 civilized life, experts in nutrition would say that, on what amounts to a purely meat diet, I'm heading for trouble. Perhaps I am. I've hunted the island for greenstuff – I've eaten things which taste like brown paper – but there's not a gourd, not a berry, not a leaf which seems to be the right stuff. 30

* The author's dog.

38

Never mind. In the inhabited islands of this group, people live on much the same diet that I'm existing on. The extras are simply bread, rice, sugar, tea, coffee and pumpkins. Theoretically, their own diet is dangerously deficient in fruit and vegetables. But the fact is that the health record of those people living on the fringe of the world – *35* children, too – is such that there is hardly, if ever, an urgent case demanding an operation. It's just as well because there's no doctor.

It moves me to wonder how many of the diseases people contract in great cities are the consequence of stress and worry and hurry rather than the result of bugs, or food going down the wrong way. Whatever *40* befalls me here, it won't be a coronary thrombosis.

Many things are becoming clearer to me as I settle down to this new way of life. Most habits – like drinking, smoking, four meals a day – are habits of environment. If you're thrown into a completely new environment, it's no effort to do without any of them. At least, that's *45* the way I feel now. There's a bottle of brandy in my tin trunk which certainly wouldn't have survived long if I was based in my London flat. As it is, I haven't the slightest inclination to take a nip from it.

I remember how astonished I was, when I searched out the aboriginal bushmen of Africa, to find how little they needed to *50* support their own way of life. They have no use – and neither have I in this place, except for the personal lift it gives me – for a permanent shelter. All the bushmen build are rough huts, beehive huts made of bent sticks, to provide cover in their overnight camps, not for the young and healthy, but for the aged and the dying. All they carry are *55* their bows and poisoned arrows to kill meat, and ostrich shells to cache their water. For the rest, the family eats when one of them brings down an antelope or a giraffe. For snacks, they eat roots and caterpillars, and probably other insects as well. They wash in oil, like coconut oil, squashed out of a seed. *60*

When I look at this entry later, I suspect that I'll think that, in my present mood, I am arguing myself right. Could be. To redress the balance, here's a list (it's been fun making it) of the things I look forward to most when I get back to civilization. It's significant what everyday things they are: *65*

1 A clean pocket handkerchief.
2 A hot bath in fresh water.
3 Soap; for preference, scented with eau de cologne.
4 A shave and a haircut.
5 A pair of pyjamas. *70*
6 Boiled silverside of beef, with carrots, dumplings and jacket potatoes.
7 (And not least) a woman's voice.

But there are compensations. This is the first time that I've passed a fortnight on earth without hearing an internal combustion engine. *75*

Lionel and Mary Jackson

The first time, too, that days have passed without a glimpse of the written word. I wonder what's happening in the world. I'll make a forecast that when I enter it again, however exciting the headlines in the newspapers in the interim, everything will be exactly the same.*

From *After You, Robinson Crusoe—A Practical Guide for a Desert Islander.*

---

1 a   (i) Who was Robinson Crusoe?
  (ii) We reveal ourselves, sometimes unintentionally, in our diaries. What sort of person does the author seem to be, judging from this entry?
  (iii) What lessons is the author learning on the island?

  b   (i) Diaries are usually private. What reader(s) has Macdonald Hastings in mind as he writes?
  (ii) The author leaves the reader to make certain **inferences.** What do we **infer** from
'that wretched disc-jockey in my head is off the air' (l. 8)
'Whatever befalls me here, it won't be a coronary thrombosis' (ll. 40–41).
'I am arguing myself right' (l. 62).

2   With a friend, read some extracts from *'Robinson Crusoe'* to the class. **Compare** the extracts with Macdonald Hastings diary entry.

3 a   Write diary entries for your fifteenth and forty-fifth days on a desert island.

  b   The author's references to 'civilized life' (ll. 24–25) and 'civilization' (l. 61) might make us ask 'What *is* civilization?' List some points you might hear in a discussion on this **topic.**

---

* Wrong as I was about many matters, I was right about that.

14 Capital Punishment
Various authors

A

Sir, It is surely time the voice of a potential victim was heard.

I am in my late seventies, I have a heart condition and I could make no resistance to an intruder who murdered me for whatever meagre sum he could find in the house.

I want the death penalty restored for my protection and for the   *5* protection of elderly disabled people, young girls, children and policemen.

The police, who are in the front line, want the death penalty restored and who would dare to deny them the right to their opinion?

Execution need not be by hanging. Emotive talk about the rope is   *10* simply an attempt to establish prejudice.

Smug, high-minded people, safe themselves, refuse even to consider a measure that might save many lives. They are, and mean to remain, out of contact with reality, wrapped in their delicate consciences.

The Methodist Union has said that a return to the death penalty   *15* would be a return to barbarism.

The barbarism is already here.

Yours faithfully,

K. H. OLDAKER,

4 Summit Close, N 14.   *20*

July 3.

B

Sir,—I have read and heard various opinions on the subject of capital punishment, and I would like to say that it is a deterrent. I as a convicted murderer can say that I would not have committed the crimes I did if capital punishment had then been in force.   *25*

Hence, today two people would have been alive; their families and mine would not have suffered the accompanying grief and sorrow; I would not have the pained conscience I have; and I would not have a recommended natural life sentence to serve.

When a murder is committed because of the absence of capital   *30* punishment, the abolitionist is as responsible for the murder as the murderer; and I accept my responsibility for what I did.

Capital punishment would most certainly protect the lives of both the potential victims and the potential murderers, plus their families and everyone concerned in such matters. A vote of Yes* means life for   *35*

(B)

* In the debate in Parliament on the Bill to reintroduce capital punishment for certain categories of murder. The Commons voted against the Bill.

41

many people in the future; a vote of No* means death and sorrow.
(Name supplied)
H M Prison
Parkhurst
Isle of Wight   *40*

C

Sir,—Were Parliament to reintroduce the death penalty, all
categories of people in or associated with the prison service would
necessarily have a part to play in its implementation. Let no one shy
away from the detail of it.

Prison governors would be responsible for requisitioning the rope,   *45*
the pinioning apparatus, the special cap placed over the prisoner's
head, and the bag of sand needed to test the drop.

The medical officer would have a duty to sign the death certificate,
having kept the prisoner at the peak of health.

The clerk of works would have to oil the gallows, civilian workmen   *50*
dig the grave and, in the context of cold-blooded bureaucratic
execution, the chaplain would, somehow, have to talk of God's
mercy.

Prison officers would have to sit with the prisoner round the clock,
test the rope, lead him to the trap-door, and ultimately, take down his *55*
body, burn his clothing and bury the corpse.

And the board of visitors would have to attend the prisoner,
consider his requests for visits and, as the group responsible for the
independent oversight of the prison, be present at the execution.

We have not had time to consult the views of our membership but   *60*
we, the officers of the Association of Members of Boards of Visitors,
would not be prepared to be party to a system geared to such barbaric
acts, and we do not think Parliament has the moral right to brutalise
prison staff by requiring such duties of them.—Yours faithfully,
Andrew Macfarlane, Mike Smith, Rod Morgan, Jane Blom-Cooper.   *65*
Association of Members of
Boards of Visitors,
Bath, Avon.

D

Sir,—Supporters of the death penalty convey the impression that
murderers are treated leniently. Life imprisonment is in reality a very *70*
severe punishment. Following a long and indefinite period in prison,
the prisoner is released on licence for life, and is subject to recall to
prison at any time. Effectively the sentence never ends.

About 800 people would have been executed since 1965 if the death
penalty had been generally available for murder. Most have not, and *75*
will not, kill again. Murder is rightly viewed as the gravest of crimes,
but this association believes that a humane approach must recognise

that rehabilitation is possible, and that even most of those who have
killed can return to society safely to lead a useful and responsible
life.—Yours faithfully,   *80*
Jenny Kirkpatrick.
National Association of Probation Officers,
London SW11

A letter to *The Times*, 6 July, 1983; **B** Letter to the *Guardian*, 7 July
          1983; **C–D** Letters to the *Guardian* 13 July 1983.

―――――――――

1 **a** (i) Which letters in this group are for the death penalty and
              which against?
          (ii) Which letter seems to you the best one, considering the
              purpose the writers have in mind?
          (iii) What is meant by 'deterrent' (l. 23) and 'rehabilitation' (l.
              78)? Why are these **key words** in the subject area?
    b 'Smug' (l. 12), 'barbarism' (ll. 16 and 17), 'cold-blooded' (l. 51),
        'bureaucratic' (l. 51), 'barbaric' (l. 62) and 'brutalise' (l. 63) might
        be described as **emotive language**.
          (i) Do you consider that such expressions strengthen or weaken
              the author's **argument**?
          (ii) Suggest other **examples** of such **language** we might meet in a
              discussion on capital punishment.
2   In groups:
    a Have one or two students re-read each letter, noting any points
        they think strong or weak.
    b Decide whether you agree or disagree that the death penalty
        should be brought back in Britain.
3   After a nuclear war a group of about 2000 people escape to an
        uncontaminated island where they hope to start a new life. A
        'parliament' of twenty of the people meets to try and draw up
        some laws on punishment. Write the discussion they might have
        on the question of the death penalty.

15 Reducing the Racket
H. F. Wallis

Many people's notion of hell would be some kind of bedlam. Few, I suspect, would see it as absolute quiet. Yet man has become conditioned to accept a certain level of noise and would probably be driven just as crazy by complete silence as by a devilish din.

Noise has been defined, in fact, as any *unwanted* sound, and it is 5
clear that in this respect attitudes can change with time. For instance, trains make quite a lot of noise, but recent research has shown that people have come to accept the conventional sounds, though not those made by the new diesels. On the other hand, soft sounds, like the scampering of mice, can be most disturbing to some. 10

City dwellers become used to higher sound levels than their rural counterparts. The sounds themselves are also of a different nature. Townsfolk are thus frequently disturbed by the comparative peace of the countryside. Some cannot bear it. With noise levels rising sharply in the towns and not-so-sharply in the countryside in recent years, the 15
differences have become more acute, so that one finds even short-term visitors to rural retreats taking their noise with them in the form of transistor radios and seeking out noisy spots for picnics, like the verges or traffic islands on busy main roads. Some people have to keep their radios on all the time while they are at home. It seems a kind of 20
neurosis.

Advances in sound-deadening techniques have made it possible to reduce noise in offices to almost nothing, but firms which have created such conditions for their executives have received no thanks. On the contrary, there have been so many protests that they have either had 25
to reduce the insulation or to introduce noise through tape recorders or electronic sound generators.

Certain kinds of noise are beneficial. Music, for instance, not only soothes the savage breast but also increases productivity. The sounds of nature are generally soothing. Recordings of surf on the seashore, 30
the rustle of trees or corn and the song of the birds are played in sanatoria and mental homes. The lullaby is as old as time.

American research has suggested that music may even produce bigger crop yields. Maize grown in a hothouse in which music was played around the clock was found to grow faster and to have 20 per 35
cent heavier stalks than maize grown in an identical hothouse without the music. It has been suggested that sound energy may increase the molecular activity of the soil, raising its temperature and influencing micro-organisms. Sounds have also been used to control pests.

On the other hand, much noise can be regarded as a form of 40
pollution. It can cause mental and physical disturbance. Cotton
workers, riveters, building workers, pneumatic drill operators and
anyone subjected to noisy machinery over long periods is liable to
sustain hearing loss. Research at Southampton University has
suggested that no fewer than 100,000 workers might be entitled to 45
compensation for hearing damage if it were included under industrial
injury benefits. Young 'pop' fans have been found to have the hearing
of the middle-aged. Traffic and aircraft noise can also hamper work in
hospitals and schools.

The Russians have found that the noise produced by a jet plane can 50
kill bee larvae and has a depressant effect on adult bees. It is said that
if you place a carnation near a radio set and turn the set on at full
volume it will wither. (I haven't tried this myself.) Noisy milking
machines and even noisy milkmaids are stated to have caused lower
milk yields and to reduce weight gain in pigs. 55

Investigations in Russia and elsewhere have revealed that noise can
not only affect the human ear but can also cause many diseases,
including cardiovascular afflictions. Its psychological effects –
irritation, loss of sleep and so on – are well known. Cases have been
recorded where abrupt noise has caused blindness, stammering and 60
even epileptic fits. Where the background level is too high, warning
noises cannot be heard and this may lead to accidents, breakdown of
machinery and so on.

Town and countryside are becoming ever noisier. Traffic roars
along motorways and through city streets; bigger and bigger jets 65
thunder and whine overhead, and soon the sonic boom may
reverberate; noisier machinery invades factory and farm; and diesel
trains trumpet like herds of charging elephants. Life whirls along
faster and faster, and the noise grows louder and louder.

It is disturbing more and more people. The Wilson Committee, 70
which reported on the noise problem in 1963, referred to a survey
showing that more than twice as many people were disturbed by noise
in 1961 as in 1948, and who can doubt that the trend has continued to
rise? In fact a survey by *The Observer* in 1971 found that city noise had
grown 50 per cent louder in nine years. 75

From *The New Battle of Britain*

1 a   (i) Which noise do you most dislike?
       (ii) Which would be more likely to 'drive you crazy' – 'complete
            silence' or 'a devilish din' (ll. 1–4)?
       (iii) Do you like or dislike the 'comparative peace of the
            countryside' (ll. 13–14)?

(iv) Do you approve or disapprove of transistor radios played out-of-doors?

(v) 'Much noise can be regarded as a form of pollution' (ll. 40–41). If so, what has it in common with other forms of pollution?

(vi) The book containing this extract was written in 1972. Do you think the author would think that the 'racket' had been reduced since then, or not?

b (i) 'Some people have to keep their radios on all the time while they are at home. It seems a kind of neurosis.' (ll. 19–21). Which sentence is **fact**, which **opinion**? Do you agree with the opinion?

(ii) It might be said that there is a **contradiction** between the beginnings of the second and fifth paragraphs. Say why you think there is or is not.

(iii) What have these pairs of words in common: sound/noise; kill/murder; determined/stubborn; information/propaganda?

2 Your youth club plans to hold an all-night open-air disco to raise funds for Vietnamese orphans. At a planning meeting various **points of view** on the project are expressed. Decide which people would attend the meeting and improvise the discussion they might have.

3 Denise is a girl in a story whose adventures take her from noisy to quiet surroundings (or vice versa). Write two 'extracts' from the story showing the **contrast** between the two environments and what Denise feels in each case.

16 The Lonely Wasteland
Peter Dunn

Peter Dunn meets a victim of inner-city devastation.

1 Knocking down the old terraced houses of central Liverpool must have seemed a good idea at the time. In place of the two-ups-two-downs with tin baths hanging in their little back yards, the city fathers showed the people the future, mostly from high rise flats with bathrooms. The result, as everyone now knows, was not urban   *5* renewal so much as a tarted up form of institutional decay. Neighbourhoods were not revitalised. They were unwittingly yet systematically destroyed.

2 One side of Penrhyn Street, off Scotland Road, survived the planners' voracious blitz. The row of terraced cottages, with their brightly   *10* painted fronts, is a reproof to an area of seedy shopping precincts, brick council flats and littered roads.

3 Most of the old tenants have died or moved away. Mr Malloy, at number 17, the street's knocker-upper who also fixed watches and clocks, has long gone. The cobbler down Oswald Street across the   *15* road is remembered only as "a foreign gentleman with a limp". Mrs Greaves, who kept the corner shop, is dead. When women in the street became pregnant they always said it was because the old lady who sold firewood bundles had put the eye on them.

4 Mrs Gibbons knows better than most that the great neighbourhood   *20* upheaval of the fifties caused casualties. As a part-time home help she visits two of them in their council tower blocks. "I've had these two old people five years," she says. "My duty's to see they're kept warm and have something to eat. Honestly, it's living hell for them because one's on the eighth floor of J. F. Kennedy Heights and is house-   *25* bound. She's in that flat morning, noon and night, year in year out, and that's the story of her life after rearing three children."

5 Even in the little enclave of Penrhyn Street cottages Mrs Gibbons' own social life consists largely of memories.

6 "I was born in this house 57 years ago and raised five children here,"   *30* she says. "In those days you'd go to the front door each side and natter an hour, taking to the neighbours. We didn't go anywhere. We didn't have the money. Now you just don't see anyone. When I've said 'good morning' to women at the new flats over the road they've

not wanted to know. You just say to yourself 'don't say it any more,   35
Pat'.

7 "My husband George works all day from 6 am till 7 pm. I come home
from work at 1 pm, the door's shut and that's it. Maybe, it's me that's
changed. One time, people would knock at the door and borrow this
or that. I've even lent someone a mop, that's the truth. And a piece of   40
soap. But it's not like that now. People can't go out for a walk at night
because of the muggings. When George takes his car round to the
garage, he takes his rings off and puts his money on that table before
he goes out.

8 "One time, you'd get together in each other's houses and have a   45
laugh. We never drank but we'd be up to 2 am talking of old times.
We used to put the children early to bed on Fridays and Saturday
nights. I'd take my stool to the front door, Sarah next door would
have hers and Mary further down and we'd chat and laugh and we'd
eat bacon ribs or pig's feet outside.   50

9 "I don't know how to put this, because we weren't rich though we
always worked, but when my mother got this house we were classed
as being well off because we had a bathroom. People would say
'lovely house. Must have plenty of money.' All the girls I went to
school with used to love me to bring them home and show off the   55
bathroom. I'd even let them come here weekends, and have a bath.

10 "My mother was very well known for her kindness. The way it
showed was if someone in the street wasn't well. She'd take them pea
soup or a bread pudding. She didn't always think of the family inside.
She thought of people outside as well.   60

11 "People don't look after their houses as much as they used to. When I
was young we'd keep a table in the back yard and we'd take it out
once every holiday to scrub our bricks outside. We used a little bit of
soda. No soap. All the neighbours would say 'How do you get your
bricks red like that?' and my mother always said to us, 'Don't tell   65
anyone what I put in the water'."

12 Mrs Gibbons remembers only one trouble family in the street. "The
father worked on the tugboats. They were the first people in the street
I knew to have a phone, one of them that hung on the wall.

13 "They were a nice family, a smashing family, but he liked his drink on   70
a Saturday night, and he'd come home and throw them all out. We'd
get the police but he never let them in. We'd put the family up, one to
a house, till next morning."

14 In a once-thriving Catholic community, even attitudes to death seem
to have become subordinated to the tedium of life on the dole.   75

15 "Years ago," says Mrs Gibbons, "if anyone close to you died, you'd
bring them home for a wake and all the neighbours would come in
and sit around and you'd be up all night, then someone else, the next
night. But now when someone's died you get taken out of the house

to such and such funeral parlour. You can't go to people anymore *80*
and say 'I'm sorry'."

From *Sunday Times*, 12 December 1982

_____

1 **a** (i) 'Things aren't what they used to be,' we sometimes hear.
            Mention three or four things which, according to the author,
            have changed for the worse in central Liverpool.
        (ii) What general idea underlies Mrs Gibbons' reminiscences of
            the past?
        (iii) The **journalist**, Peter Dunn, probably asked Mrs Gibson a
            series of questions as the **interview** proceeded. Suggest
            questions which might have preceded paragraphs **6**, **7**, **8**, **9**,
            10, **11** and **15**.
   b By study of the **context** and/or discussion, try to give the meanings
        of these words from paragraphs **1** and **2** which you may find
        difficult:

        high-rise flats; urban renewal; institutional decay; revitalise;
        unwittingly; voracious; blitz; reproof.

2 Suppose the various organisations in your district are having a
   'Help the Lonely Ones' week. By discussion decide
   (a) What organisation does your group belong to?
   (b) Who are the loneliest people in our society?
   (c) Why are they lonely?
   (d) What should be done to help them?
   A short list of recommendations should be the result of your
   discussions.

3 A writer of social history will often give detailed accounts of
   people's lives at different periods. Write an account of a typical
   day in the life of Mr Malloy (l. 13) *or* Mrs Greaves (ll. 16–17) *or*
   Mrs Gibbons (ll. 28–81) *or* Mrs Gibbons's mother (ll. 57–66) as a
   social historian might describe it. Some library **research** into
   social history will help in this assignment.

17 Not My Kind of Place
Paul Theroux

The author, touring Scotland, had found Cape Wrath and Sutherland strangely appealing. But Aberdeen was a different matter.

We reached the coast. Off-shore, a four-legged oil-rig looked like a mechanical sea monster defecating in shallow water. It was like a symbol of this part of Scotland. Aberdeen was the most prosperous city on the British coast – the healthiest finances, the brightest future, the cleanest buildings, the briskest traders. But that was not the whole 5
of it. I came to hate Aberdeen more than any other place I saw. Yes, yes, the streets were clean; but it was an awful city.

Perhaps it had been made awful and was not naturally that way. It had certainly been affected by the influx of money and foreigners. I guessed that in the face of such an onslaught the Aberdonians had 10
found protection and solace by retreating into the most unbearable Scottish stereotypes. It was only in Aberdeen that I saw kilts and eightsome reels and the sort of tartan tight-fistedness that made me think of the average Aberdonian as a person who would gladly pick a half-penny out of a dunghill with his teeth. 15

Most British cities were plagued by unemployed people. Aberdeen was plagued by workers. It made me think that work created more stress in a city than unemployment. At any rate, this sort of work. The oil industry had the peculiar social disadvantage of being almost entirely manned by young single men with no hobbies. The city was 20
swamped with them. They were lonely. They prowled twilit streets in groups, miserably looking for something to do. They were far away from home. They were like soldiers in a strange place. There was nothing for them to do in Aberdeen but drink. I had the impression that the Aberdonians hated and feared them. 25

These men had seen worse places. Was there in the whole world an oil-producing country that was easy-going and economical? "You should see Kuwait," a welder told me, "You should see Qatar." For such a man Aberdeen was civilisation. It was better than suffering in an oil-rig a hundred miles offshore. And anyone who had been in the 30
Persian Gulf had presumably learned to do without a red-light district. Apart from drinking and dancing Scottish reels there was not a single healthy vice available in Aberdeen.

50

It had all the extortionate high prices of a boom town but none of
the compensating vulgarity. It was a cold, stony-faced city. It did not   *35*
even look prosperous. That was some measure of the city's mean
spirit – its wealth remained hidden. It looked over-cautious, un-
welcoming and smug, and a bit overweight, like a rich uncle in dull
sensible clothes, smelling of mildew and ledgers, who keeps his wealth
in an iron chest in the basement. The windows and doors of Aberdeen   *40*
were especially solid and unyielding; it was a city of barred windows
and burglar alarms, of hasps and padlocks and Scottish nightmares.

The boom town soon discovers that it is possible to make money
out of nothing. It was true of the Klondike where, because women
were scarce, hags came to regard themselves as great beauties and   *45*
demanded gold dust for their grunting favours; in Saudi Arabia today
a gallon of water costs more than a gallon of motor oil. In Aberdeen it
was hotel rooms. The Station Hotel, a dreary place on the dockside
road across from the railway station charged £48 a night for a single
room, which was more than its equivalent would have cost at The   *50*
Plaza in New York City. Most of the other hotels charged between
£25 and £35 a night – fifty bucks on average, and the rooms did not
have toilets. I went from place to place with a sense of mounting
incredulity, for the amazing thing was not the high prices or their
sleazy condition but rather the fact that there were no spare rooms.   *55*

For what I calculated to be $40 I found a hotel room that was like a
jail cell – narrow and dark, with a dim light fifteen feet high on the
ceiling. There was no bathroom. The bed was the size of a camp cot.
Perhaps if I had just spent three months on an oil rig I would not have
noticed how dismal it was. But I had been in other parts of Scotland,   *60*
where they did things differently, and I knew I was being fleeced.
To cheer myself up I decided to go out on the town. I found a joint
called Happy Valley – loud music and screams. I thought: Just the
ticket.

But the doorman blocked my path and said: "Sorry, you can't go   *65*
in."

Behind him were jumping, sweating people and the occasional
splash of breaking glass.

"You've not got a jacket and tie," he said.

I could not believe this. I looked past him, into the pandemonium.   *70*

"There's a man in there with no shirt," I said.

"You'll have to go mate."

I suspected that it was my oily hiker's shoes that he really objected
to, and I hated him for it.

I said: "At least I'm wearing a shirt."   *75*

He made a monkey noise and shortened his neck. "I'm telling you
for that last time."

"Okay, I'm going. I just want to say one thing," I said. "You're
wearing one of the ugliest neckties I've ever seen in my life."

Up the street another joint was advertising "Country and Western *80*
Night." I hurried up the stairs, towards the fiddling.
"Ye canna go in," the doorman said. "It's too full."
"I see people going in," I said. They were drifting past me.
"And we're closing in a wee munnit."
I said: "I don't mind." *85*
"And you're wearing a wrinkled jacket," I said. "And what's that,
a gravy stain?"
"Ye canna wear blue jeans here. Regulations."
"Are you serious? I can't wear blue jeans to an evening of country
and western music?" *90*
"Ye canna."
And so I began to think that Aberdeen was not my kind of place.
But was it anyone's kind of place? It was fully-employed and tidy and
virtuous, but it was just as bad as any of the poverty-stricken places I
had seen – worse, really, because it had no excuses. The food was *95*
disgusting, the hotels over-priced and indifferent, the spit-and-
sawdust pubs were full of drunken and bad-tempered men – well,
who wouldn't be? And it was not merely that it was expensive and
dull; much worse was its selfishness. Again it was the boom town ego.
Nothing else mattered but its municipal affairs. *100*

From *Sunday Times*, 7 August 1983

---

1 **a** (i) Say why 'The boom town ego' (l. 99) might make a
suitable subtitle for this extract.
(ii) What points in the extract might most annoy Aberdonians?
(iii) Do you agree that 'kilts and eightsome reels and . . . tartan
tightfistedness' are 'the most unbearable Scottish
stereotypes' (ll. 11–13)?
(iv) Theroux's writing often makes us 'sit up and think'. What
ideas does he suggest by:
(a) 'Aberdeen was plagued by workers' (ll. 16–17)
(b) 'there was not a single healthy vice available in Aberdeen'
(ll. 32–33)
(c) 'none of the compensating vulgarity' (ll. 34–35)
(d) 'it is possible to make money out of nothing' (ll. 43–44)?
(v) Should Theroux have been allowed into 'Happy Valley' or
the 'Country and Western Night'?
b Some people might say that Theroux, in this extract, is making
value judgments (personal opinions based on little evidence). How
far do you agree with this comment?
2 Make a tape-recording of the **dialogues** in the passage, using
appropriate voices.
3 Write about a place you dislike, in the Theroux **style**.

18 They Danced for Joy
Nadine Gordimer

Toby Hood, a young Englishman, is sent to Johannesburg as the representative of his family's publishing firm. He is received by both black and white communities. One night he finds himself at a crowded African party in Sophiatown, a black township.

There was a little breeze of notes on a saxophone; it died down. A clarinet gave a brief howl. Somewhere behind the press of people, the big bass began to pant. Music grew in the room like a new form of life unfolding, like the atmosphere changing in a rising wind. Musical instruments appeared from underfoot; people who had been talking   5
took to another tongue through the object they plucked or blew. Feet moved, heads swayed; there was no audience, no performers – everyone breathed music as they breathed air. Sam was clinched with the piano in some joyous struggle both knew. A yellow youth in a black beret charmed his saxophone like a snake, with its own weaving   10
voice. The bass thumped along for dear life under the enchanted hand of a man with the bearded, black delicate face of an Assyrian king. A fat boy with a pock-marked face jumped with rubber knees into a little clearing; girls began to swing this way and that from their partners' hands, like springs coiling and uncoiling.   15
I had seen jazz-crazy youths and girls at home in England, in a frenzy of dance-hall jive. I had seen them writhing, the identity drained out of their vacant faces, like chopped-off bits of some obscene animal that, dismembered and scattered, continue to jig on out of nervous impulse. But the jazz in this room was not a frenzy. It   20
was a fulfilment, a passion of jazz. Here they danced for joy. They danced out of wholeness, as children roll screaming down a grass bank. Now and then a special couple would make space for themselves, and gather the whole swirling vigour of the room into their performance. They laughed and shouted to the others who   25
danced around them, corollary to their rhythm; comments and challenges flew back.
One of the men in business suits came up to me and said confidentially, 'I suppose this must all seem rather crude.'
'Crude?'   30
He waved a hand at the room, that buffeted him where he stood, so that he had the stance of a man on a ship in a high sea.
'My friend,' I said, 'you don't know what our parties are like.' And it was true that that very first night I was struck by the strange innocence of their dancing. In all its wild and orgiastic shake and   35

shamble, there was never a suggestion that it was a parody of or a substitute for sex. There was none of the dreamy concupiscence that hangs, the aura of a lean, wolfish sex-hunger, about the scarcely moving couples in a white night-club. For these people, the music and the dancing were not a dream and an escape, but an assertion. Once or *40* twice I took one of the young women in their bright nylon blouses and danced, but it was more than my own lack of skill and half-hearted experience of dancing as a rather embarrassing social necessity that made me feel almost as if I were maimed in that press of dancing people. It was more than my stiff, shy, and unwilling limbs. What was *45* needed was – at a deeper level – something akin to the feeling I had had when I was swimming with Stella Turgell at Mombasa, the feeling that the age-old crystals of the North were melting away in my blood. The men and women about me had had little to drink, they had none of the trappings of food and ease without which the people among *50* whom I had lived are unable to whip up any sort of mood of celebration; yet it was there, spontaneously. Their joy was something wonderful and formidable, a weapon I didn't have. And, moving feebly among them, I felt the attraction of this capacity for joy as one might look upon someone performing a beautiful physical skill which *55* one has lost, or perhaps never had. Lopped off, gone, generations ago; drained off with the pigment fading out of our skin. I understood, for the first time, the fear, the sense of loss there can be under a white skin. I suppose it was the point of no return for me, as it is for so many others: from there, you either hate what you have not *60* got, or are fascinated by it. For myself, I was drawn to the light of a fire at which I had never been warmed, a feast to which I had not been invited.

From *A World of Strangers*

---

1 **a** (i) Cover the passage and check how many **details** you can remember about what Toby (the **narrator**) sees, hears and feels.

(ii) From your own experience of a dance or disco, mention details of what you saw, heard and felt.

(iii)

White or English parties	*Black or African parties*
'jazz crazy youths'	'a fulfilment'
'writhing'	'a passion'
'identity drained out of vacant faces'	

Use words and **phrases** from the passage to continue these lists, which show the **contrast** Toby feels between two sorts of dancing.

      (iv) Say whether you think Toby is being fair to the dancers described in the left hand column in Question 1a(iii).

      (v) Why does Toby mention 'drink', 'food' and 'ease' in lines 49–50?

      (vi) Read lines 45–63 again and say what Toby feels the Africans have got that he lacks.

  b The writer uses some interesting **imagery**.

      (i) Find the **similes** in lines 14–15 and 17–20; and the **metaphors** in lines 47–48 and 61–62 and say how these help to **emphasise** the main **theme** of the passage.

      (ii) Find four other **examples** of metaphors and similes and say how they add to the interest of the passage.

2 With your group, prepare a project on the **topic** of dancing. Collect details, pictures and musical illustrations about dances from different periods and places, e.g. (a) where, when and why the dance took place; (b) what the dancers actually do; (c) what the dance represents or depicts. Present your topic to the class.

3 Imagine that one of Toby's African friends visits Britain and spends an evening in a dance hall or disco. Write the letter he might send home describing this experience.

*So you hate
Christmas? Is it more
trouble than it's worth? Well,
you won't convince* **Sue Arnold,**
who says . . .

19 I Vote We Have Christmas More Often!

You're right of course. It's vulgar, it's commercial, it's expensive, it's over-long, over-crowded, over-rated and light years removed from the original theme of shepherds abiding and cattle a-lowing. But it's Christmas and I love it. No other occasion in the year is so loaded with excitement or generates so much energy and enthusiasm. *5*

I am prepared to defend the last shopping day, the last mince pie, the last plastic nose jettisoned by the last unexploding Christmas cracker against all those carping critics who complain that Christmas is a rip-off. It may be, but what's most important is that this is the time, the only time, when families traditionally get together – and *10* that's what makes it a special time of year for me.

Don't misunderstand me. I love the wrapping paper and razmataz as well. As a newspaper reporter I daresay I see more razmataz at Yuletide than most, because it's round about now that news editors are racking their brains for new angles on robin redbreasts ankle- *15* deep in gleaming white snow.

Last year I was sent out to interview Father Christmases in West End department stores. One Oxford Street Santa told me the cautionary tale of the jolly old Santa in the store next door who'd been caught shop-lifting. Apparently he'd put all the stolen goods *20* into his toy sack for safe-keeping, and would certainly have got away with it had not one sharp-eyed seven-year-old piped up loud and clear, 'Mummy, why has Santa got two bottles of whisky and a rack of gold watches in his sack?'

Aha, crowded shops, cry the Scrooges among us, now that's another *25* awful thing about Christmas. Well, don't go into them if you dislike crowds. Do what I do. Buy your presents throughout the year and keep a bottom drawer constantly on the go ready for December.

But I love crowds. I'm one of those odd bods who gravitate towards them like rabbits to headlights. I'm a sucker for sales for that very *30* reason. I never buy much; I just like mass hysteria. Besides, shops at Christmas look so pretty, with bits of holly dangling from the cornflakes packets and snowmen lurching drunkenly off all the lights.

What I especially like is the devil-may-care recklessness that gets   *35*
into people at this time of year. 'Well, it only comes once a year,' says one man ordering half a pint of perfume for his wife. If it does this sort of thing for people, I vote we have Christmas more often!

Every book you read about planning for Christmas says in bold black type at the start that the secret of a good Christmas is to **be**   *40*
organised. Codswallop! I love Christmas because it's so disorganised – in our house at any rate. The fun for me is to do things you wouldn't dream of doing any other time, like eating Chinese figs for breakfast or opening three boxes of chocolates all at the same time. We have lunch *after* the Queen's speech so that everyone has   *45*
ample time to open, play with and break their toys as well as work up a healthy appetite.

One Christmas in a fit of enthusiasm I bought a fat paperback from Waterloo Station enticingly called *Coping with Christmas*. What an extraordinary manual! Starting from January, it told you exactly   *50*
what you should be doing every day of the year to prepare for 25 December. Thus on 17 February it was time to sugar the almonds or steep the peaches in brandy, on 9 August you were to check for holes in the stockings, on 18 October you were dispatched to the attic to test the Christmas tree lights and – would you believe? – on Boxing Day,   *55*
when I'm invariably in a state of hung-over collapse, I was expected to trip nimbly into the kitchen and start stirring *next* year's Christmas pudding. But Christmas isn't like a military campaign. It's a gas. The chores connected with it like stirring cakes and decorating trees are a *pleasure*.   *60*

If you're a dyed-in-the-wool traditionalist Christmas is ideal, because it positively bristles with tradition. Apart from the big public traditions like the Oxford Street lights, there are the private traditions that every family cherishes. As a child we would always walk home from morning service via the golf course and dozens of neighbours   *65*
who plied us with punch and salted almonds.

I couldn't bear to be married to the kind of millionaire who flies the family to a five-star hotel in Mombasa for Christmas. The idea of eating turkey and plum pudding in a bikini is plain ridiculous.

I have this self-consciously misanthropic friend who announced to   *70*
everyone last December that he was going to spend Christmas Day alone, in bed, eating baked beans listening to Mozart's *Requiem Mass* and reading *Hard Times*. His resolution failed him. He came round at midday, joined us for lunch and in fact was the linch-pin of the charades and party games in the evening.   *75*

I don't believe people who say they don't like Christmas. It's like saying you don't like laughing.

From *Living*, December 1981

1 **a** (i) Who is the 'You' in the opening sentence?
   (ii) The author likes Christmas for various reasons. List as many of her reasons as you can find.
   (iii) The author speaks of doing 'things you wouldn't dream of doing any other time' (ll. 42–43). Mention five such 'things' you do or would like to do at Christmas.
   (iv) A 'Brain of Britain' could answer these questions – can you?
       (a) What does the word Christmas really mean?
       (b) Where do we hear about 'shepherds abiding' and 'cattle a-lowing' (l. 3)?
       (c) What is the origin of the word 'Yuletide' (l. 14)?
       (d) How, according to legend, did the robin get its red breast?
       (e) What is Santa's full name and how did he get it (l. 18)?
       (f) Who was Scrooge (l. 25)?
   (v) Why do you think the 'misanthropic friend' behaved as he did (ll. 70–75)
 b (i) The article has a number of **colloquial** words and phrases like 'racking their brains' (l. 15) and 'odd bods' (l. 29). Find three other examples of this sort.
   (ii) Is the article serious or humorous? Say why you think so.

2 With a partner write and tape the rest of this telephone conversation. Invite others to listen to one voice only and guess the rest:
'And the prices! Thirty-nine ninety-five for a Baby Bubbles doll – mind you it will drink real water and, well, it's a bit embarrassing really . . . '
'That's nothing. Do you know what I paid for a Biotechnic Man? Sixty-two pounds! But of course, Jerry next door's getting one, so . . . '
'That's just it. These kids are spoilt out of their minds. Why do we bother with Christmas?'

3 Write a short letter or radio talk or magazine article or diary entry about Christmas by a very young person, a very old person, a person not of the Christian religion or yourself in the future. If you do not celebrate Christmas, write a piece describing an annual festival important in your religion to someone unfamiliar with it.

20 Witches
Alison Uttley

When we crept softly through the woods, keeping on the soft places between the stones, making our zigzag way without a word, we were placating the witches which haunted the dark places, which were prepared to leap out at us at nightfall. Nobody told us about witches, we knew without any speech, and when we heard the story of Hansel   5
and Gretel who wandered through a wood such as ours and found a cottage in the depths we expected to find the same little house made of ginger-bread crisp and golden, with sugar plums on the roof and almond rock on the roof. We knew we couldn't resist such dainties, we should eat and be captured. There was no escape from witches   10
except the sign of the cross. I did not discover this talisman until I was older, for we were an evangelical family. When I went to school I met my first witch. She was an old woman in a red shawl and she muttered to herself as she walked along the country road.

'Run! Run!' cried the children. 'She's a witch! She will catch you   15
and take you home and eat you.'

So I ran faster than I had ever run before, and I expected the witch to fly on wings after me. Nothing happened, but I kept a wary eye for her. She could change me into a cat or a fox or a hare I was told, and I believed this.   20

All this was secret, unknown to parents, a strange legend which passed from infant mouth to infant mouth, a tale of witchcraft, come down through the centuries. It must be true, I argued to myself. It was in a book, my fairy tale book, and in a poem by Burns I heard, and all books and poems were gospel truth. A witch could put a little girl in a   25
circle, and there was no getting free from that boundary. In daytime I did not mind, I rather enjoyed the excitement of running from a witch, but at night it was different. A witch had flaming eyes and she could see when I could distinguish nothing. She lay in wait in my bedroom, behind the door on a winter's night. She clothed herself in a dressing-   30
gown or a petticoat, which hung on the door, and she waited for me to close my eyes. I could see her eye glint in the light of the fire. In the morning she was only a brass hook on the door but that was her changed shape, her deceitful concealment from grown-up people. They said she was a hook; I knew she was a witch and laughter would   35
not dissuade me. I did not talk about her for this gave her extra power over me.

There were witches in the Bible, and I heard of them in Church where I felt safe and content. The Witch of Endor, whom I saw with a pointed hat on her grey hair, carrying a wand, which she turned to the   40

Lionel and Mary Jackson

ground, to summon up the spirits of the dead. Dark glittering eyes,
curved chin and nose, and quick nervous voice belonged to a witch, a
skinny hand and claws for fingers. Adults did not speak of witches,
they said they did not exist nowadays, but once upon a time it was
different. Then they told strange tales, which would be explained now   *45*
by psychology, a split personality, hypnotism, good and evil lurking
in one body, a psychopath.

Science seeks for unity in nature, laws obeyed by forces, mathema-
tical exactitude in the play of behaviour, and witches who work
against known laws will not be tolerated. Yet I think there was some   *50*
potent reason for the belief in witches, which was current until a
century ago. The belief is still alive, say some people who pry into old
superstitions and seize on haphazard careless talk by the older
country people. This talk is then help up to ridicule, and disdain. 'We
who know better than they', is an attitude of ignorance. It should be   *55*
'We do not know, we cannot explain such things by any known laws,
but the world changes, and new laws are discovered which may throw
a light on these strange happenings in the future.' For the superstitions of one era are the science of another.

From *Wild Honey*   *60*

1 **a** (i) What is a witch?
    (ii) Why were witches usually women?
    (iii) Alison Uttley was clearly an imaginative child. Choose five or
    six **details** from the passage which illustrate this.
    (iv) Which childhood experience of your own is nearest to those
    described by the author?
   b (i) Choose one of the five **examples** given in lines 45–47 and say
    how it might explain a 'strange tale from the past'.
    (ii) The **theme** of witches runs through the passage but is treated
    differently in the last paragraph. Say what the difference is.
    (iii) Can you think of examples to support the **statement** in the
    last sentence?
2 **a** The author says that there was 'some potent reason for the belief
   in witches' in past times (ll. 50–51). Decide by discussion which
   one or more of these reasons would explain that belief:
    (i) Witches were mentioned in the Bible
    (ii) Witches with evil powers really existed
    (iii) People in the past had little idea of science
    (iv) Old women looked like witches
    (v) A witch was someone to blame when things went wrong.

b Make a recorded **anthology** entitled *Witchcraft*. You could include selections from Shakespeare's *Macbeth*, Burns' 'Tam O' Shanter,' Ainsworth's *The Lancashire Witches*, Miller's *The Crucible*, an African novel like Achebe's *Things Fall Apart* and many other sources. A short introduction to each piece would be helpful for the listeners.

3   WITCHCRAFT IN THE VILLAGE
                          Woman's Withered Arm

A wave of fear has hit the tiny Loamshire hamlet of Lower Newton, scene of a prolonged witch-hunt 243 years ago.
Shopkeeper Eileen Aldiss is convinced that the strange condition of her right arm is caused by . . .
Complete this newspaper report from the *Loamshire Herald* for 6 October 1985.

21 The Legend of the Kraken
Lucy Berman

Are there such things as sea-serpents? Is there a Loch Ness Monster? People have argued for centuries about the existence of strange creatures in lakes and seas. Sea-monster legends have grown up in every seafaring nation. Some creatures once believed to be legendary have been proved to have a basis in fact. One of these creatures was *5*
the *kraken*.

The kraken was a huge monster, first described by Norwegian writers. In 1555, Olaus Magnus wrote: 'Their Forms are horrible, their Heads square, all set with prickles, and they have sharp and long horns round about, like a Tree rooted up by the Roots . . . one of *10*
these Sea-Monsters will drown easily many great ships provided with many strong Mariners.'

Two hundred years later the legend had become greatly exaggerated. A fair-sized kraken was said to be one-and-a-half miles in circumference! Stories were told of sailors who landed on a kraken, *15*
believing it to be an island. They settled themselves for the night and built a fire, whereupon the monster sank below the surface, leaving them to swim for their lives.

Erik Pontoppidan, an eighteenth century Norwegian bishop, described the kraken surfacing: 'At last several bright points or horns *20*
appear, which grow thicker and thicker the higher they rise above the surface of the water, and sometimes they stand up as high as the masts of middle-sized vessels. It seems these are the creature's arms, and, it is said, if they were to lay hold of the largest man-of-war, they would pull it to the bottom.' *25*

One account of the kraken legend was that there were only two of these creatures. They were said to be as old as the world and to be doomed to die and to rise to the surface on the day that the world ended. The more usual accounts, however, claimed an innumerable population of krakens in the sea, which was an ever-present danger to *30*
sailors.

At the beginning of the nineteenth century, a French naturalist named Denis de Montfort described how a kraken (which he called a *poulpe colossal* or 'colossal octopus') wrapped its arms around a three-masted ship and nearly succeeded in pulling it to the bottom of *35*
the sea. He had no evidence for this story other than a picture on a church wall, but he used his imagination and invented a struggle in which the crew only just saved themselves by cutting off the monster's arms. His story was a sensation, and its success prompted him to even wilder imaginings. He published an account of the sinkings of ten *40*
ships in a single night by a whole school of *poulpes colossal*.

No one believed this second account. Both de Montfort and the kraken were discredited. In 1861, however, a real ship named the *Alecton* had a real encounter with a kraken. The animal tried to keep at a fair distance from the ship, but the captain decided to harpoon it. *45* He managed to tie it to the side, but it broke away, leaving a portion of its tail behind. It was described as having a body fifteen to eighteen feet long, and a head with a parrot-like beak surrounded by powerful arms five to six feet in length. The arms were equipped with strong suckers, and the captain felt that a close encounter with these arms *50* could be very dangerous. His men wanted to pursue the creature in a small boat, but he refused.

When the *Alecton* story was published, few people could doubt it. The evidence was very detailed and supported by many witnesses. The captain of the *Alecton* declared that he had seen Denis de Montfort's *55* *poulpe colossal*. He said that it was not a myth, but was in fact a giant-sized squid. Seafaring people were quite familiar with small squids. They recognized easily the slender body, the head with its sharp beak surrounded by eight arms and two longer tentacles. But previous to the *Alecton* incident, accounts of giant squid-like creatures had been *60* relegated to the realms of myth and fancy.

It was not until the early 1870's that the existence of the giant squid was accepted as fact by scientists. From about 1870 to 1879, giant squids by the dozens were stranded off Nova Scotia. Scientists were able to measure and classify actual specimens. The largest one found *65* measured fifty-seven feet overall, including tentacles forty-nine feet three inches in length. The scientists also studied accounts of the kraken and the *poulpe colossal*, and they concluded that the legendary and the real creatures were one and the same animal.

From *The Creepy Crawly Book*

---

1 **a** (i) What is a monster? Which is your favourite monster?
   (ii) Which is more interesting, the legendary creature (the Kraken) or the real one (the giant squid)?
   (iii) Why were people in the past so ready to believe in monsters?
   b (i) Sometimes a passage contains a number of words which emphasise the main **theme**. Say which of the following words from the passage are **thematic** in this way:
   existence, strange (l. 2); legendary (l. 4); tree (l. 10); surface (l. 17); account (l. 26); die (l. 28); claimed (l. 29); evidence (l. 36); church (l. 37); discredited (l. 43); captain (l. 45); doubt (l. 53); witnesses (l. 54); slender (l. 58); previous (l. 59); myth (l. 61).
   (ii) With Question 1**a**(ii) in mind, suggest an alternative title for the extract.

2 a The Norwegian Bishop (l. 1) and the French naturalist (l. 32) used their imaginations to make up stories about the Kraken. Use your imagination to make up a group story about a Kraken, one person beginning, another continuing, and so on.

  b Rehearse and tape-record Tennyson's poem 'The Kraken.'

  c Read John Wyndham's novel *The Kraken Wakes* and prepare extracts to read aloud to the class, explaining how each fits in to the story.

3 Suppose that the Loch Ness Monster is finally found and identified. Write a feature article for a newspaper describing the earlier 'sightings', the actual discovery and a scientific account of the creature. Include suitable headlines and sub-headings.

22 Wilfred Owen's Ghost
Aidan Chambers

Wilfred Owen was one of England's finest poets; no one has better written about the horror of war than he. And it was a tragedy of war that killed him on 4 November 1918, only a few days before the First World War came to its end. By ironic mischance his family learned of his death on the very day of the Armistice, 11 November. His brother, Harold Owen, was at that time in the Royal Navy, a lieutenant serving in the light cruiser, HMS *Astraea* which was on station in tropical waters off Africa. 5

Lt Owen was very depressed, quite unable to enter into the happy mood felt by most people at the good news of the war's end. He thought he was suffering from the heat and the weakening effects of malaria. Nevertheless, he also felt something was wrong, something he could not quite identify. He was restless, uneasy, even thought of sending home a telegram asking whether his brothers Wilfred and Colin were well. But he decided against doing anything; the feeling was too vague. 10

15

It was in this 'mood' that Harold Owen saw his brother Wilfred's ghost some time *before* news of Wilfred's death reached him. The experience is described in the third volume, *War*, of Harold Owen's biography, *Journey from Obscurity*. 20

I had gone down to my cabin thinking to write some letters. I drew aside the door curtain and stepped inside and to my amazement I saw Wilfred sitting in my chair. I felt shock running through me with appalling force and with it I could feel the blood draining away from my face. I did not rush towards him but walked jerkily into the 25 cabin – all my limbs stiff and slow to respond. I did not sit down but looking at him I spoke quietly: 'Wilfred, how did you get here?' He did not rise and I saw that he was involuntarily immobile, but his eyes which had never left mine were alive with the familiar look of trying to make me understand; when I spoke his whole face broke into his 30 sweetest and most endearing dark smile. I felt no fear – I had not when I first drew my door curtain and saw him there; only exquisite mental pleasure at thus beholding him. All I was conscious of was a sensation of enormous shock and profound astonishment that he should be there in my cabin. I spoke again: 'Wilfred, dear, how can 35 you be here, it's just not possible . . .' But still he did not speak but only smiled his most gentle smile. This not speaking did not now as it had done at first seem strange or even unnatural; it was not only in some inexplicable way perfectly natural but radiated a quality which

65

made his presence with me undeniably right and in no way out of the   *40*
ordinary. I loved having him there: I could not, and did not want to
try to, understand how he had got there. I was content to accept him;
that he was here with me was sufficient. I could not question anything,
the meeting in itself was complete and strangely perfect. He was in
uniform and I remember thinking how out of place the khaki looked   *45*
amongst the cabin furnishings. With this thought I must have turned
my eyes from him; when I looked back my cabin chair was empty . . .

I felt the blood run slowly back to my face and looseness into my
limbs and with these an overpowering sense of emptiness and
absolute loss . . . I wondered if I had been dreaming, but looking   *50*
down I saw that I was still standing. Suddenly I felt terribly tired, and
moving to my bunk I lay down; instantly I went into a deep oblivious
sleep. When I woke up I knew with absolute certainty that Wilfred
was dead.

Harold Owen's story is one among many of a similar kind recorded   *55*
by hundreds of people over many years. Whether he actually saw the
returned spirit of his brother or whether the apparition was some kind
of telepathic communication from his distressed family, or indeed
whether it was none of these but simply a vivid waking dream brought
on by the tropical heat and Mr Owen's uneasy feelings and   *60*
wonderings about his brothers, everyone must decide for themselves.

From *Great Ghosts of the World*

---

1 a (i) What replies might you get if you asked several people 'What
is a ghost?'
(ii) Harold Owen does not use the word 'ghost' in his **account** of
what he saw. Say why you think this is.
(iii) Check the meaning of 'involuntarily immobile' (l. 28)
and say why Harold uses it to describe Wilfred.
(iv) Why does Harold feel no fear (l. 31)?
(v) How could Harold 'know with absolute certainty that
Wilfred was dead' (ll. 53–54)?
  b Most people would agree that Harold Owen's account of his
experience is very striking. Say which features of **theme** and
language help to make it so.
2 a Ask some people you know if they have seen a ghost. Record or
write down their answers.
  b With a friend, practise reading aloud (i) the author's introduction
(ll. 1–20) and conclusion (ll. 55–61); (ii) Harold Owen's account
of what he saw. Listen carefully to each other's reading, discuss
ways of bringing out the strangeness of the experience and tape-

record the passage as if for radio.

c The author offers three explanations (ll. 56–61) for Harold Owen's experience in his cabin. In groups discuss which explanation you would support, or whether any other explanation is possible.

3 Jane's cousin Bryan is keen on weekend gliding. One Saturday Jane is in the attic sorting out old photographs. She sees Bryan near the door. She speaks to him. He waves to her and she feels her breath frozen in her body. That evening she hears that Bryan has had a fatal accident.

Write Jane's account of her experience.

23 Are We Being Watched
Janet and Colin Bord

THE WITNESSES WHO RAN AWAY . . .

How would you feel if you were out walking one day and you suddenly came across a landed UFO and entities? Many people would naturally be frightened and run away. This was the reaction of a 15-year-old boy and girl who had a strange experience near Kolmarden in Sweden on 23 August 1967. About dusk they saw a reddish glow 5 moving over some nearby woods, and as they walked past an old hut they saw lights moving around it. Soon they saw a large round light hanging in the air near a relative's house; and then they heard a whistling sound and footsteps. All of a sudden a small entity about 4 feet 4 inches (130 centimetres) tall jumped out from behind a bush. It 10 had a large head, dark piercing eyes, and its arms and legs were very thin. As the two witnesses ran off in fright, they saw it lift a box-like object with a tube protruding from it. Next day deep three-toed footprints were found by the boy.

Two 10-year-old girls, Fiona Morrison and Karen McLennan, also 15 wanted to escape when they saw a UFO entity. But who of us would have stayed to watch when the entity began to walk towards us? Fiona and Karen live at New Elgin in Moray, Grampian, Scotland, and at 6.30 p.m. on 18 May 1977 were playing in fields near their homes. Hearing a strange humming noise in the woods, they went to 20 investigate, and saw a 30-foot (9-metre) cylindrical object with a dome on top. It looked like polished metal, and no doors or windows could be seen. There was a red light on the dome, and a rotating red band around the body of the UFO. It was hovering just above the ground and the girls could see a 'man' beside it. Although he was 25 partly in the bushes, they could see that the figure was tall and thin and dressed in silver. As he began to move towards them the girls ran away. But they stopped and looked back, and saw that the entity had gone. The UFO began to take off, which it did in steps by moving left, rising, moving left, rising, moving left and finally rising vertically very 30 fast.

. . . AND THOSE WHO STAYED TO WATCH

The witnesses in the last two cases still had time to note interesting features of the UFO events even though they ran away. Those witnesses who are too curious to run away, and have hidden themselves somewhere without the UFO entities noticing them, have 35 seen even more interesting details of the entities' behaviour. Fifteen-year-old Adilon Batista Azevedo witnessed a strange UFO landing on 26 July 1965 at Carazinho in Brazil. That evening, while on his way to the cinema, he saw two UFOs land not far away. He hid behind a low wall and saw three entities come out of one craft and two out of the *40* other. They were about 5 feet (1.5 metres) tall and wore helmets and dark one-piece suits. One carried a bright object that looked like a wand. The entities talked together for about five minutes in a strange sibilant language and then they walked around their UFOs, bending down as if examining the craft. Then they re-entered them and took *45* off at speed.

Adilon had a bad headache for five days afterwards, which may have been caused by his being too close to some unknown radiation given off by the UFOs. It is safer, therefore, to watch a UFO landing from a building, as did 14-year-old Carlos Alberto do Nascimento. *50* He was at work in Rio de Janeiro, Brazil, on 24 November 1967 when at 2.30 p.m. he heard a high-pitched sound and saw a UFO apparently landing among trees. He called a colleague and they watched as three entities dressed in white came out of the UFO as it hovered just above the ground. They walked about in a strange way, *55* with their arms unmoving by their sides, and this went on for several minutes before they went under the UFO. Twenty-five minutes after the landing, the two witnesses went outside and saw that the UFO was still there, but five minutes later it had gone. Next day they visited the landing-site with a friend and found that the grass had been trampled *60* and a tree burnt. The most interesting discovery was that the grass was tall, and would have covered the witnesses if they had tried to walk through it. The entities they had seen walking in the grass had been visible down to their knees, which suggests that they were not walking on the ground but somehow moving above it. *65*

From *Are We Being Watched?*

---

1   a   (i)   What is a UFO? And what is an 'entity'?

           (ii)   Why are 'witnesses from different countries' included in the passage?

         (iii)   Do you think the writers of the passage believe in UFO's and 'entities'? Do you?

         (iv)   Do you think it likely or unlikely that 'entities' would resemble humans in shape?

         (v)   If UFO's exist, where do they come from and why do they come?

   b   This passage raises the question of **evidence**. What do we mean by evidence? How do we decide if evidence is reliable or not?

2   Script and tape a radio interview with two or three of the 'witnesses' mentioned in the passage. You will need a presenter to introduce the topic at the beginning and 'sign off' at the end; the interviewer and the witnesses.

3   a   Read the following newspaper report by Alan Hamilton, Woodbridge, from *The Times* of 3 October, 1983. Write a letter to *The Times* giving your views on UFO's and 'entities':

Down to earth approach to a UFO

The mission was to seek a close encounter, preferably of the third kind, but any kind would do.

The place was a vast clearing deep in the 10,000 acres of Aldewood Forest, Suffolk, where, according to yesterday's *News of the World*, an alien spacecraft landed at Christmas, 1980, flew among the trees, left imprints on the ground, and vanished only when the United States Air Force from Woodbridge base, half a mile away, came out to investigate.

Witnesses, according to the paper, have since greatly elaborated on the event, speaking of beings in silvery suits who practised levitation.

The first being encountered yesterday was clad in corduroy trousers and black wellingtons. He came, he said, not from outer space, but the Forestry Commission. His name was not the Mekon, but Vincent Thurkettle.

The second being closely resembled a collie dog, and was too busy chasing sticks to levitate.

"This is the site", said the first being, gesturing around a rough acreage of stumps and twigs.

"When the UFO is supposed to have landed the whole area was covered by Corsican pines 75ft tall and only 10ft apart. It would have taken a fair feat of navigation to get among that lot."

He pointed to indentations in the ground that might have been made by the feet of a far-travelled craft. "Rabbits", he said. "They dig for roots."

But, surely, the searchers reported burn marks on the surrounding trees and radiation in the ground?

"The burns were the marks we put on the trees for felling. And as for radiation, a craft from outer space is going to use a far more sophisticated form of propulsion."

A third being, who said he was David Boast, and a gamekeeper, was quoted in the *News of the World* as saying how cattle panicked near his house on the night in question. "There are no cattle anywhere near here", he told me. "This is a forest."

Neither the first nor the third being could recall anything untoward on the night in question, except that it was Christmas.

   b   Describe your own actual or imaginary encounter with a UFO and its 'entities'.

24 'Stop the Fighting!'
Alan Burgess

Gladys Aylward, a Christian missionary in China, receives an official order to go to the town prison, where a riot has broken out.

They hurried up the road in through the East Gate. A few yards inside the gate the blank wall of the prison flanked the main street. From the other side came an unholy cacophony: screams, shouts, yells, the most horrible noises.

"My goodness!" said Gladys, "it certainly is a riot, isn't it?"   5

The Governor of the prison, small, pale-faced, his mouth set into a worried line, met her at the entrance. Behind were grouped half a dozen of his staff.

"We are glad you have come," he said quickly. "There is a riot in the prison; the convicts are killing each other."   10

"So I can hear," she said. "But what am I here for? I'm only the missionary woman. Why don't you send the soldiers in to stop it?"

"The convicts are murderers, bandits, thieves," said the Governor, his voice trembling. "The soldiers are frightened. There are not enough of them."   15

"I'm sorry to hear that," said Gladys. "But what do you expect me to do about it?"

The Governor took a step forward. "You must go in and stop the fighting!"

"I must go in . . . !" Gladys's mouth dropped open; her eyes   20 rounded in utter amazement. "Me! Me go in there! Are you mad! If I went in they'd kill me!"

The Governor's eyes were fixed on her with hypnotic intensity. "But how can they kill you? You tell everybody that you have come here because you have the living God inside you. . . ."   25

The words bubbled out of the Governor's mouth, his lips twisted in the acuteness of distress. Gladys felt a small, cold shiver down her back.

"The—living God?" she stammered.

"You preach it everywhere—in the streets and villages. If you   30 preach the truth, if your God protects you from harm, then you can stop this riot."

Gladys stared at him. Her mind raced round in bewilderment, searching for some fact that would explain her beliefs to this simple, deluded man. A little cell in her mind kept blinking on and off with an   35

urgent semaphore message: "It's true! You have been preaching that
your Christian God protects you from harm. Fail now, and you are
finished in Yangcheng. Discard your faith now, and you discard it for
ever!" It was a desperate challenge. Somehow, she had to maintain
face. Oh, these stupidly simple people! But how could she go into the   *40*
prison? Those men—murderers, thieves, bandits, rioting and killing
each other inside those walls! By the sounds, louder now, a small
human hell had broken loose. How could she . . . ? "I must try," she
said to herself. "I must try. O God, give me strength."

She looked up at the Governor's pale face, knowing that now hers   *45*
was the same colour. "All right," she said. "Open the door. I'll go in
to them." She did not trust her voice to say any more.

"The key!" snapped the Governor. "The key, quickly."

One of his orderlies came forward with a huge iron key. It looked
designed to unlock the deepest, darkest dungeon in the world. In the   *50*
keyhole the giant wards grated loudly; the immense iron-barred door
swung open. Literally she was pushed inside. It was dark. The door
closed behind her. She heard the great key turn. She was locked in the
prison with a horde of raving criminals who by their din sounded as if
they had all gone completely insane. A dark tunnel, twenty yards   *55*
long, stretched before her. At the far end it appeared to open out into
a courtyard. She could see figures racing across the entrance. With
faltering footsteps, she walked through it and came to an abrupt
standstill, rooted in horror.

The courtyard was about sixty feet square, with queer cage-like   *60*
structures round all four sides. Within its confines a writhing, fiendish
battle was going on. Several bodies were stretched out on the
flagstones. One man, obviously dead, lay only a few feet away from
her, blood still pouring from a great wound in his scalp. There was
blood everywhere. Inside the cage-like structures small private battles   *65*
were being fought. The main group of men, however, were watching
one convict who brandished a large, bloodstained chopper. As she
stared, he suddenly rushed at them and they scattered wildly to every
part of the square. He singled one man out and chased him. The man
ran towards Gladys, then ducked away. The madman with the axe   *70*
halted only a few feet from her. Without any instinctive plan, hardly
realising what she was doing, she took two angry steps towards him.

"Give me that chopper," she said furiously. "Give it to me at
once!"

The man turned to look at her. For three long seconds the wild dark   *75*
pupils staring from bloodshot eyes glared at her. He took two paces
forward. Suddenly, meekly, he held out the axe. Gladys snatched the
weapon from his hand and held it rigidly down by her side. She was
conscious that there was blood on the blade and that it would stain
her trousers. The other convicts – there must have been fifty or sixty   *80*
men cowering there – stared from every corner of the courtyard. All

action was frozen in that one moment of intense drama. Gladys knew
that she must clinch her psychological advantage.

"All of you!" she shouted. "Come over here. Come on, form into a
line!" She knew vaguely that the voice belonged to her, but she had 85
never heard it so shrill. "Get into line at once. You, over there! Come
on, form up in front of me!"

Obediently the convicts shambled across, forming into a ragged
group before her. She regarded them stormily. There was silence.
Then suddenly her fear had gone. 90

"You should be ashamed of yourselves," she said, berating them
like an irate mother scolding a crowd of naughty children. "The
Governor sent me in here to find out what it was all about. Now, if
you clean up this courtyard and promise to behave in future, I'll ask
him to deal leniently with you this time." She tried to keep her eyes 95
away from the still figures of the dead. "Now what is your grievance?"
she snapped. "Why did you start fighting like this?"

From *The Small Woman*

1 a (i) 'I'm only the missionary woman' (ll. 11–12). What are
Gladys's unspoken thoughts here?

(ii) Why does Gladys stammer when she says 'The—living God?'
(l. 29)?

(iii) Why is 'beliefs' (l. 32) a **key word** in the paragraph which
begins at line 33?

(iv) Think of examples from history of people who have suffered
for their beliefs. Would you do the same? If so in what kind of
situation?

(v) Explain how a moment when 'all action was frozen' could
also be one of 'intense drama' (ll. 81–82)?

b (i) Gladys's change of attitude is **emphasised** by the author's
choice of words and **phrases** e.g. 'a small, cold shiver' (l. 27)
compared with 'her fear had gone' (l. 90). Describe this
change of attitude and find other words and phrases which
help the reader to appreciate it.

(ii) The author uses **graphic detail** (e.g. 'his mouth set into a
worried line' (ll. 6–7); 'a huge iron key' (l. 49). Find further
examples of such detail and show how two of them help the
writer in his purpose.

2 In your groups discuss a likely **sequel** to Gladys's action in
quelling the riot. Here are some clues, actually taken from the next
few pages of the book, to help you:

'Now go over in that corner and appoint your spokesman'

. . . . . .

Unless their friends or relatives sent in food, they starved.

. . . . . .

They never saw the outside world, women or the mountains, a tree in blossom or a friendly face.

. . . . . .

The Governor bowed to Gladys.

. . . . . .

'You must find them occupations.'

3   A British **journalist** hears about the events in the prison and **interviews** Gladys. Write the article he or she might send in to his or her newspaper, including some points about Gladys Aylward's character and beliefs. Supply a suitable title.

25 Suffering
Harold Loukes

Do you think it is a cruel thing that God should let people die?

'If everyone . . . there wouldn't have been enough room in the world for everybody because the population is increasing, so somebody has to die off.'

That is true enough, but Christine, what about somebody who dies 5
young or dies tragically? What is natural is that old people should die
and so on, but when a baby dies at birth for example, if a boy of 21 dies,
do you think that is terribly unfair on God's part?

'No, because he might have been in misery for the rest of his life.'

'I think that is stupid. Because he might have been a great man, too, 10
he might have been anything. I don't think God, if there – there can't
be a God or he wouldn't let them die like that. It's just one of those
things that somebody gets killed.'

'Maybe God wants him for something else in heaven.'

Well, now, this is I think the real question. This one about the 15
unfairness of the world if you are going to believe in God, and in a God of
love, so I think we have all probably got something to say about this.
Beryl, you haven't said anything yet. Let's hear your voice. Do you think
it is unfair that there should be this suffering and fear in the world?

'Yes.' 20

Now, can we think of different kinds of suffering. I mean a child dies
of polio, or a young man was killed in an aeroplane crash. Now is there a
difference between these two?

'His body gives way on one part, and on the other part . . . Oh but
he has had good health, but something else killed him.' 25

Yes?

'It is accidental the crash he had in the plane.'

But polio is not accidental?

'No.'

No. We haven't quite got the difference yet, but we are getting warm. 30
What other difference is there between somebody who just dies of polio
and a young man who just takes up an aeroplane and crashes? There is
one very important difference.

'The chap who has crashed in the aeroplane is killed instantly; well,
the person who has got polio isn't. It may be years before he dies.' 35

Yes, I think that is an important difference, but it isn't the one I am
thinking of . . .

'When a man goas up in the aeroplane he just takes the risk doesn't
he, but the other person can't help it.'

Yes, that's it Trevor. That's the real difference. The man chooses to   40
*go up in the aeroplane and he chooses to climb a mountain and falls over
the edge, or whatever it is. He is using his freedom, isn't he? It's not true
of the polio. Now do you think having freedom is a good thing or a bad
thing?*
'It's a good thing.'   45
Why?
'Well, you can do what you want to.'
*And you would rather have the power of doing what you want to do,
even if it means you do wrong things?*
'I dunno.'   50
'You learn by things you do wrong. You learn and then next time
you do them right.'
Is that always true?
'Well, in most cases.'
And you would take the risks, would you? I mean, you realize that   55
there are risks in giving anybody freedom?
'Yes, yes.'
And you would take the risks?
'Hmmm.'

From *Teenage Religion*

1   a   (i) Why does the adult ask so many questions?
          (ii) The extract contains several **examples**. Give two more
              examples like that of the child with polio and two like that of
              the young man in the aeroplane.
        (iii) The conversation suggests links between God, suffering and
              freedom. Can you say what the links are?
        (iv) What are the risks referred to near the end of the passage?
    b   (i) The conversation reflects various **viewpoints**. Which of these
              viewpoints in the passage would you support:
              (a) 'He might have been in misery for the rest of his life' (l. 9)
              (b) 'He might have been a great man, too' (ll. 10)
              (c) 'Maybe God wants him for something else in heaven' (l.
                  14)
        (ii) Which of these viewpoints (not in the passage) do you think
              the adult speaker would support:
              (a) 'God loves people even when he allows them to suffer'
              (b) 'God must be a cruel God'
              (c) 'We are fated to die at a certain time – why bother about
                  freedom?'
              (d) 'Because we have free will we have the choice of doing
                  right or wrong.'

2 a Arrange speakers for the different voices in the extract and tape-record the discussion.

b Listen to the tape-recording and continue the discussion in your group, if you can.

3 'You learn by things you do wrong. You learn and then next time you do them right.'

From your own experience or knowledge write a short piece to **illustrate** or **disprove** these remarks.

26 Spike Milligan Protests
Spike Milligan

To: His Holiness The Pope,
The Vatican   *21st October, 1976*

Your Holiness,
    A couple of years ago I wrote to you regarding a Professor White in America who carries out awful experiments on animals, and I said   *5* unless the Church could make a definite decision about ex-communication or not, that I myself could not go on being a Catholic whilst such a crime was being committed.
    My letter was eventually passed to Cardinal Heenan who wrote to me, alas with no positive decision about what the Church should do.   *10* In the face of this, I have decided I cannot be a Catholic any longer.
    I wish to take up the Buddhist Faith.

I have the Honour to remain,
your Holiness's most devoted and
obedient servant.   *15*

SPIKE MILLIGAN

In reply, Spike had a noncommittal answer from John Crowley at Archbishop's House, London

12th November, 1976

Dear Mr Crowley,   *20*
    Thank you for your letter, but it doesn't do anything positive. Years ago I reported the horrendous experiments of Professor White, and I feel helpless in the face of these so called 'scientific experiments', and when I discovered the man was a Catholic, I was horrified some approach had not been made to him by a Catholic in an authoritarian   *25* position. He should be ex-communicated, alas he hasn't been and my efforts to bring pressure on him, via the Church, have failed and, therefore, it's no good staying with a very large Regiment, holding rifles, when none of them, in fact, have any ammunition.
    Therefore, I intend to withdraw from the Roman Catholic faith; it's   *30* a very sad decision to make, but as Hamlet once said 'a good idea must give way to a better one' and my better one will be Buddhism.
    Thanks for writing.

Sincerely,

SPIKE MILLIGAN

From *The Spike Milligan Letters.*

1 a (i) 'All animals are equal, but some are more equal than others' (Orwell: *Animal Farm*).
Do you think that the human animal is equal to or superior to the other animals?
(ii) What kind of 'experiments' (l. 5) has Spike Milligan in mind?
(iii) Who, according to Spike, should be excommunicated, and why? What does excommunication mean?
(iv) Why do you think Spike talks of taking up the Buddhist faith?
(v) Why was John Crowley's answer 'noncommittal' (l. 17)?
(vi) What is meant by 'rifles' and by 'ammunition' (l. 29)?
b Here is a poem by Spike Milligan. Do you think Spike makes his point better in the letters or the poem?

Open Heart University

We've come a long way
     said the Cigarette Scientist
as he destroyed a live rabbit
     to show the students how it worked.
He took its heart out
     plugged it into an electric pump
     that kept it beating for nearly two hours.

I know rabbits who can keep their hearts
     beating for nearly seven years
And look at the electricity they save.

2 a *Either* 'Was Spike wise or foolish?' Hold a class discussion on this question. The **chairperson** should come armed with relevant facts and figures, like this item in *The Scotsman* of 19 July 1984:

Anger over vivisection statistics

The number of experiments on live animals fell by 14 per cent last year to the lowest level since 1959, the Home Office Minister, Mr David Mellor, announced yesterday.

The drop of 600,000 experiments to 3.6 million during 1983 was dramatic and very welcome, he added. But the National Anti-Vivisection Society gave warning of an angry reaction by animal rights campaigners.

The number of animal experiments in 1983 was 35 per cent lower than the highest recorded annual total of 5.6 million in 1971, according to Home Office statistics. More than 80 per cent of last year's experiments were on mice and rats. Less than 1 per cent were on cats and dogs, and less than 9 per cent on rabbits and guinea pigs.

The number of experiments involving cosmetics was down 4 per cent to 18,000 representing 0.5 per cent of the total. The ban on using cats and dogs in smoking experiments – imposed in 1976 – continued to be enforced.

"This most welcome reduction in live animal experiments indicates a real desire on the part of the scientific community to reduce the number of experiments and to seek alternatives wherever possible," said Mr Mellor. But animal experiments were necessary to make medical and scientific advances and to ensure that products were safe.

Mr Brian Gunn, general secretary of the NAVS, said: "We are appalled that our so-called civilised society still permitted 3.6 million animal experiments in 1983 despite all the animal rights groups have done to highlight the desperate plight of laboratory animals and the strong public reaction against such experiments."

He said that unless meaningful action were taken soon, it would not be possible to contain the anger of the movement's activists.

or **b** Read this piece from the introduction by Norma Farnes to *The Spike Milligan Letters*. Then tape a telephone dialogue between Spike and Norma.

For example, no matter what the situation is at the office, and I mean by that any form of crisis – and we have at least four a day – the birds must be fed. That in itself needs an explanation. Spike has a small balcony at the back of his office, and every day he feeds the birds, and he has names for them all. I can understand the pigeons are quite tame, but he has tamed the sparrows that come there, and they literally eat out of his hands. His favourite sparrow is Fred, that's because Fred is always last to catch on that the food is there, so Spike waits to see he gets his fair share. His favourite pigeon is Hoppity, because he's got something wrong with his foot, and every day they come to his balcony and he carries on a conversation with them. I still remember, and this always sticks in my mind, Spike opening the windows one New Year's day, and saying 'Happy New Year Lads'. On the balcony Spike has window boxes, and towards the end of the summer, only last year, he kept two wasps alive for weeks, by putting a spoonful of jam inside a jar, turned on its side, so they could get to it.

3 Write a letter to Spike Milligan on the **topic** of animal experiments.

27 Released
J. C. Hampe

A young fisherman from the west coast of Jutland wanted to dive
into the water while bathing; but he hit his head on a stone and was
drowning, having lost consciousness. He rose to the surface twice
but went down again before he could be rescued. In these moments
his whole life passed in front of him. First of all he felt completely   *5*
deserted. Then he laid hold of God's grace and was drawn out
again, a new man.

Again and again, people (especially those who can tell of a swift,
violent death) relate in astonishment with what extreme vividness the
life panorama opens up before them. Many similar experiences, of a   *10*
kind familiar to mountaineers, lie behind the account of the Austrian
Hias Rebitsch. He was climbing the south face of the Goldkappel in
South Tyrol, a rope-length ahead of his companions, secured by three
pitons. An overhanging rock was still between him and his goal. He
thought he had surmounted it, when a piton came loose and he fell   *15*
backwards into the abyss in a break-neck drop:

I still grasp completely what is happening, am fully conscious of what
is going on round me: I am brought up short for a moment. I register:
the first piton has gone. The second. I strike against the rock, scrape
against it as I go down, want to resist, to claw at it. But a wild power   *20*
dashes me inexorably down and down. Lost. Finished.
But now I am not frightened any more. Fear of death leaves me. All
feeling, every perception is snuffed out. Only more emptiness,
complete resignation within me and night round about me. I am not
plummeting downwards any more either. I am sinking softly through   *25*
space on a cloud, resigned, released. Have I already passed the
gateway to the kingdom of shadows? Suddenly light and movement
enter the darkness round me. Cloudy figures detach themselves from
me and become clearer and clearer. A film flickers on to a screen inside
me: I see myself in it again, see myself, only three years old, tottering   *30*
to the grocer's shop next door. In my hand I am clutching the penny
that my mother had given me so that I could buy myself a few sweets.
Then I see myself as an older child, see how my right leg is caught
under a falling layer of planks. My grandfather is trying to raise the
planks. Mother is cooling and stroking my crushed foot . . . More   *35*
and more pictures out of my life flicker up and are shaken into
confusion. The film snaps. Chains of light cut through the empty
black background like lightning. Catherine wheels, raining sparks,
flickering will o' the wisps . . . Again I am standing in front of myself.

I cannot recognize myself physically in this form, but I know that it is *40*
me. Suddenly a cry out of the distance: 'Hias!' and again, 'Hias!
Hias!' A call from within me? Suddenly sun-bathed rock and light
and silence before me. My eyes have opened. The window into the
past had been thrown open. Now it is shut again. And again the
frightened cry. It comes from this world, from above . . . Now I *45*
become conscious for the first time that I have just survived a great
fall, have returned from a long journey, back through my life, back
from an earlier existence, have slipped into my skin again. I worked
myself up the seventy feet with the help of the rope . . . The last piton
had held. *50*

From *To Die is Gain: the Experience of One's own Death*

1 **a** (i) Say briefly what this passage is about.
     (ii) What points in the passage are surprising?
     (iii) Study this chart and say how it might help us understand the
           passage:

Mind	Body
Mental experience	Physical experience

     (iv) What is meant by 'The film snaps' (l. 37)?
   b (i) Why is Hias's story (ll. 17–50) written in the **present**, not the
           past tense?
     (ii) Understanding the main idea of a passage helps us under-
          stand single words. Can you give the meaning of 'abyss' (l.
          16); 'register' (l. 18); 'inexorably' (l. 21); 'resigned' (l. 26);
          'survived' (l. 46)?
2 **a** Practise reading aloud this short story by W Somerset Maugham.
        Decide whether one or three speakers would be more suitable:

DEATH SPEAKS: There was a merchant in Baghdad who sent
his servant to market to buy provisions and in a little while the
servant came back, white and trembling, and said, Master, just
now when I was in the market-place I was jostled by a woman in
the crowd and when I turned I saw it was Death that jostled me.
She looked at me and made a threatening gesture; now, lend me
your horse, and I will ride away from this city and avoid my fate. I
will go to Samarra and there Death will not find me. The merchant
lent him his horse, and the servant mounted it, and he dug his

spurs in its flanks and as fast as the horse could gallop he went. Then the merchant went down to the market-place and he saw me standing in the crowd and he came to me and said, Why did you make a threatening gesture to my servant when you saw him his morning? That was not a threatening gesture, I said, it was only a start of surprise. I was astonished to see him in Baghdad, for I had an appointment with him tonight in Samarra.

b Discuss the idea which links the story and the passage 'Released'. Do you agree with the idea? If not, decide why not.

3 Write parts of the 'life panorama' you might see if you were unfortunate enough to be in a situation like that of Hans Rebitsch in the extract.

28 Is There a Life Hereafter?
Barbara Smoker

Death is generally regarded as an evil – even by people who believe in heaven. But death is essential to life. Without death there could be no birth, no evolution, no younger generations coming along, and certainly no chance of promotion! 'We should not,' said Herbert Samuel, 'see death as an injury, but rather life as a privilege.' 5

To the humanist, death is simply, as Epicurus said, the end of life. To most religious people, however, it is a transition to a better life. Indeed, it is fair to say that the doctrine of a life hereafter is the one ingredient that makes religion so popular. But this is what Bernard Shaw said about it: 'Now the man who has come to believe that there 10 is no such thing as death, the change so called being merely the transition to an exquisitely happy and utterly careless life, has not overcome the fear of death at all: on the contrary, it has overcome him so completely that he refuses to die on any terms whatever.'

Why are most people so desirous of an afterlife? They generally 15 think of it as life in a perfect world. But a perfect world would necessarily be static – and, surely, very boring!

The chief motive for belief in an afterlife is the unhappiness of being separated from those who are dear to us, particularly when the separation is the permanent one of death. But friends who meet in this 20 life after a lapse of, say, twenty years find that they no longer really know one another. Besides, living on hope is not really living; it is only marking time. To live, you have to build new personal relationships. And even if the belief in reunion gives people comfort, this is no guarantee of its truth. 25

It is also argued that, since life on earth is so unjust, there must be another life to redress the balance. But why should injustice here lead to an expectation of justice somewhere else?

I have noticed that whenever I question the existence of God, one reply I get is that this world is so wonderful it must have been designed 30 by a supreme being; but when I question the belief in an afterlife, this world is said to be so bad that there must be another one ready to put it right!

The chief *theological* argument for an afterlife is that the existence of an omnipotent God of love demands it. But this world, on the 35 religious theory, is as much God's design as any other, and if he cannot or will not prevent evil from triumphing here, why assume he can or will manage things better elsewhere? Anyway, the argument is pointless except for those who already have an unshakable belief in a God of love and justice. 40

But is personal survival after death a *possibility*? This raises the whole question of personal identity. What could survive that would still really be *you*? Your identity depends on your memories, your likes and dislikes, and all your funny little ways. These depend on a living brain, on your particular biochemistry, where you live, the way *45* in which you have been educated, and the way life treats you. And, of course, your personality, your opinions, your appearance, and your body cells all change very much during life. Supposing you were to go to heaven exactly as you were the day you were born, or as you may become by the end of a long life, would you regard that newborn baby *50* or that senile centenarian as being really *you*? If you decide that it is the genetic potential that is the real you, what about identical twins? Are they really only one person? The more you think about it, the more snags you will see.

From *Humanism*

1   **a**   (i) Why do some people wish for an after-life?
           (ii) The writer deals with the difficulties in believing in an after-life. Give in your own words any two of these difficulties.
         (iii) 'Living on hope is not really living.' (l. 22) Think about your own life and the lives of people you know and decide whether you agree with this **statement**.
        (iv) Re-read the last paragraph carefully. Then try to show what we mean by 'identity' (ll. 42, 43) and 'personality' (l. 47).

   b   (i) Sometimes we get clues to the meaning of a word from the **context**. What clues might help us guess the meaning of 'humanist' (l. 6); 'doctrine' (l. 8); 'theological' (l. 34); 'omnipotent' (l. 35)?
         (ii) The author criticises **arguments** for a belief in an after-life. Can you think of one such argument she has not considered?

2   It is usually a good idea to hear **both sides of an argument**.
   a   Write down the questions you would ask someone who believes in an after-life, and someone who does not.
   b   Interview the two people you have chosen, using the questions you have written as starting points.
   c   Give a report on the interviews to the class.

3   Write a poem, song, article or speech on *one* of these **themes**:
   a   'Live your life well, for you won't get another'
   b   'In my Father's house there are many mansions'

29 The Nature of God
Harold Loukes

'I don't think God is a person, but more a thought in our minds which we have conjured up, and it has really become true.'

'God must be a kind person who has a great power to command. I think of him as one of us, but more understanding, and a person who knows everything.'   5

'God is not visible to man. He is all that is good and kind and he lives amongst us. A God cannot be proved in our minds that is true, so we just have to have faith in him.'

'Well, I think he is a man with long white flowing robes, and hair down to his shoulders, and a long beard.'   10

'Well, I always used to think of God as a man who sits in a golden throne up above the clouds, and just sits and watches us, and sends his messengers down to us.'

What you said, is that what you used to think?

'I think it now.'   15

That is what you still think?

'Yes.'

'Well, I think near enough the same as Terence! I think he has a long beard and he sits up above with all the angels round him.'

'I imagine God as a form of superior angel.'   20

'God is abstract – when people – when – I think we would need a very atomic brain to find out about him, but I think even if the greatest scientist tried to invent something about him, they would not get the real God. Like people call God a he. Well how do we know he is a he? How don't we know he is a she?'   25

'I was going to say the same.'

Well, say it.

'How do we know that God is a man and not a woman?'

'For all we know the fish in the water and the animals might believe in a God of their own. For all we know they might go to their church   30
services amongst their little families, and they might think of God as an animal like them, and they might think of a fish, you know as a fish like them for a God.'

'Well, I have always thought of God up above the clouds in heaven.'   35

'I think we only think of God up in heaven, heaven meaning above and hell below, because we think it is a better place above than it is below – not that it really exists, but that is really in a different atmosphere altogether, or everywhere that we could not see.

'I think God is everywhere around us and he is what we say.'   *40*

From *Teenage Religion*

━━━━━━━━━━━━━━━━━

1 **a**   (i) Suggest names and ages for the speakers in this conversation.
        (ii) Which two ideas of God in this extract seem to you furthest
            apart?
        (iii) What might the speaker mean by God's 'messengers' (l. 13)?
        (iv) Could God be a woman (l. 28)?
        (v) Do you think that Heaven and Hell exist (ll. 34–39)? Say why
            you do or do not.
   b   Hearing a **phrase** like 'a man with long white flowing robes' (l. 9)
        or 'a form of superior angel' (l. 20), some people might say, 'Those
        are only **metaphors** for God'. Say what you think is meant by this
        remark.
2   Here are some questions for a class discussion:
        (a) How could we show that God exists, or does not exist?
        (b) The Greeks and Romans believed in many gods. Were their
        beliefs false?
        (c) Does believing in God make people live better lives?
        (d) If the universe came to an end, would God end with it?
3   Write the **comments** which (a) a Christian (b) a Muslim and (c) an
        atheist might make on the conversation in this extract.

Glossary

(Within an entry, heavy type indicates a related word or cross-reference. The numbers in brackets refer to extracts where the questions following include the feature listed.)

accent: the way spoken English is pronounced in different areas. The Aberdeen accent is quite different from the Cornish accent. (5)

account: narrative usually dealing with real life events. In *A Pattern of Islands* Arthur Grimble gives an interesting account of his life in the South Pacific. (22)

anthology: a collection of writings in poetry or prose. Palgrave's *Golden Treasury* is a well-known anthology of short poems. (20)

appreciation: a **comment** in speech or writing which deals with the good (and sometimes the bad) features of something. In *Kes* (B. Hines) Billy Caspar's teacher gives an appreciation of Billy's talk about training a hawk. (3)

argument: reason(s) put forward to support a **viewpoint** or **proposition**. By **both sides of the argument** we mean the reasons or **opinions** of those who support and of those who reject the proposition, e.g. 'The money spent on space travel could be used to feed the hungry nations or for health research. But space travel brings advances in scientific knowledge and the thrill of unexpected discoveries'. (14, 28)

biography: the story of a person's life, e.g. *The Small Woman* by A. Burgess. The story of a person's life written by him/herself (e.g. *Cider with Rosie* by L. Lee) is an **autobiographical account**. (6, 7)

chairperson: the person directing a meeting or discussion. 'Chairman' is now thought to be sexist in tone, so 'chairperson' is often used. (26)

colloquial: conversational; found in everyday speech, e.g: 'Get lost'; 'spud-bashing'; 'taking the micky out of . . . '. (19)

comment: a remark, spoken or written, giving a person's **opinion** of or response to something, e.g.: *A Clockwork Orange* (by A. Burgess) is a disturbing but perceptive novel. (29)

compare and contrast: show the similarities and differences between two things. We could make many comparisons between 1985 and 1984, and many contrasts between 1985 and 1685. (13, 15, 18)

context: the words or sentences near a given word or **phrase**. We learn the meanings of words by meeting them in different contexts. (16, 28)

contradiction: a **statement** in conflict with a previous point. To say 'I believe in state education but I'm sending my child to an independent school' seems to be a contradiction. (15)

criterion (plural: **criteria**): a standard by which we judge something. Houses of the future will have to meet strict criteria of heat conservation and ease of maintenance. (3)

description: a picture in words. Lawrence Durrell gives us some fascinating descriptions of animals in *My Family and Other Animals*. (7)

detail: a small part of a whole. (See also **graphic detail**.) In a good **biography** we would expect to find interesting details of the subject's life. (18, 20)

dialect: the distinctive form of speech found in a region or social class. 'Dreich' (damp and dismal), 'ginnel' (narrow passageway), 'spink' (chaffinch) and 'clout' (cloth or clothing) are dialect words from different parts of the country. (5)

dialogue: speech between two or more speakers, usually indicated by inverted commas or the speakers' names. E. Morgan's poem 'First Men on Mercury' is based on a strange dialogue between Earthmen and Mercurians. (1, 3, 9, 17)

disprove: to show that a **statement** is false. To disprove the statement 'It doesn't matter what you eat so long as you enjoy it' we could produce facts and figures linking diet with certain diseases. (25)

dramatic: exciting; with action, conflict and suspense. J. Wyndham's *The Day of the Triffids* gives a dramatic **account** of an attack on the population by horrific mobile plants. (1)

emotive language: words or **phrases** meant to persuade or shock by rousing our feelings. Such **language** is often inspired by matters of conflict or controversy in public life. (14)

emphasise: to stress. In *Brave New World*, set in the future, A. Huxley emphasises the idea that people will be specially conditioned to do the work chosen for them. (18, 24)

evidence: **facts**, etc., which help to prove something. The evidence for life on Mars is rather slight. (8, 23)

example: an instance or point **illustrating** a general idea. We might refer to the mystery of the 'Marie Rose' as an example of truth being sometimes stranger than **fiction**. (3, 5, 6, 14, 18, 20, 25)

fact/fiction: something that really exists or has happened/an invented or imagined story. The fact of the loss of the 'unsinkable' ship 'Titanic' in 1912 was foreshadowed in a work of fiction published in 1898, in which a similar ship, named 'Titan', also on its maiden voyage, struck an iceberg and sank. (1, 6, 15)

formal/informal: serious in tone or wording/**colloquial** or popular in expression, e.g. 'persons apprehended misappropriating the merchandise will suffer the consequences'. 'Anyone caught pinching the goods will catch it'. (4)

graphic detail: vivid **detail**, easily pictured in the mind. Wilfred Owen's poem 'Exposure' has some graphic details of trench warfare in the First World War. (24)

illustrate: give one or more **examples** to support or explain an idea or **argument**. We might illustrate the benefits of life in the country by mentioning the fresh air, the quietness and the friendliness of village neighbours. (25)

imagery: figurative **language**, especially **similes** and **metaphors**, e.g. 'Look like the innocent flower, But be the serpent under't' (Shakespeare). (18)

infer: to deduce a point or idea from a passage of speech or writing. We might make various **inferences** if we read that there is often violence at a certain football club. (8, 13)

interpret: explain the meaning of something. We interpret the slogan 'Four legs good, two legs bad' (in Orwell's *Animal Farm*) to mean that animals are superior to humans. (1, 3)

interview: a question and answer session with a person. People in the news, like politicians, singers and churchmen, are often asked to give radio or television interviews. (10, 16, 24)

italics: sloping type used to **emphasize** a point, e.g. 'You must check in at the flight desk *at least one hour* before take-off'. (1)

journalist: a person who writes for a newspaper or magazine. **Journalism** also includes preparing news items for radio and television. (16, 24)

key word: a word which is very important for our understanding of the **theme** of a passage or work. 'Honour' is a key word in Shakespeare's *Henry IV* and 'Gentleman' in Dickens' *Great Expectations*. (14, 24)

language: the words by which we communicate. Churchill's command of the English language was shown in his wartime radio broadcasts. (2, 14, 22)

literally: in actual **fact**. It would be absurd to say 'the team manager literally tore a strip off goalkeeper Jenkins'. (1)

metaphor: an implied **comparison** or **simile**, e.g. 'The wind was a torrent of darkness among the gusty trees, The moon was a ghostly galleon tossed upon cloudy seas' (A. Noyes). (18, 29)

narrator: the person, real or imagined, telling the story. In *Kidnapped* (R. L. Stevenson) David Balfour is the narrator, telling the story of his own adventures in the Highlands. (1, 5, 18)

opinion: one person's **view** of or idea about some matter. There are conflicting opinions about the use of animals in scientific research. (6, 8, 15)

phrase: a group of words not making a complete sentence. Many books have a striking phrase as title, e.g. *Lord of the Flies* (W. Golding); *Far From the Madding Crowd* (T. Hardy); *Crime and Punishment* (F. Dostoyevsky). (18, 19, 24, 29)

present tense/past tense: form of verb showing events happening now or conditions remaining true/form of verb showing events having happened or conditions existing previously, e.g. 'Brown takes the catch with an amazing dive to his left'/'The Owl and the Pussycat went for a sail in a beautiful pea-green boat'. (27)

proposition: a **statement** which affirms or suggests something, e.g. 'necessity is the mother of invention'. (5)

proverb: a wise saying, e.g. 'a stitch in time saves nine'; 'it's an ill wind that blows nobody any good'. (10)

research: finding out something by study or questioning, e.g. John's research showed him that half his friends were vegetarians. (4, 5, 10, 12, 16)

sequel: something resulting from or following a previous event; the next part of a story. The happy sequel to Androcles' taking a thorn out of a lion's paw (in

Shaw's play *Androcles and the Lion*) was that the lion did not eat him in the Roman arena. (24)

simile: a comparison used for **illustration** or effect, e.g. 'Just then flew down a monstrous crow As black as a tar barrel' (L. Carroll). (18)

statement: a sentence, spoken or written, expressing a **fact** or **opinion**, e.g. 'Princes Street is the finest street in Europe'. (20, 28)

style: the manner in which a writer expresses himself. Dickens often writes in a humorous style; Hemingway in a direct style. (17)

survey: a general **account** of a subject. A survey of rock music would include singers like Elvis Presley and Gene Vincent. (5)

theme: the main idea; a **topic** to write or speak about, e.g. the Prime Minister took as her theme the need to cut public spending. A **thematic** study of poetry might include a group of poems on town life. (4, 11, 18, 20–22, 28)

topic: a subject to write or speak about. The 'Any Questions' programme deals with topics of current and general interest. (6, 13, 18)

value judgments: personal **opinions** based on limited **evidence**. Saying that something is utter rubbish is often a value judgment. (17)

view, viewpoint, point of view: an **opinion**; what someone thinks of some matter; how someone sees something, e.g. big powerful cars may not appear attractive when seen from the viewpoint of the pedestrian. (12, 15, 25)

Acknowledgments

The authors and publishers wish to thank the following for permission to reproduce printed matter: Page 1, Langston Hughes, 'Thank You M'am' from *Third World Voices for Children*, ed. E. Dowell and Edward Lavitt © Allison & Busby Ltd; Page 5, Mav Franks, *Young People from Woman's Hour: A Second Selection*, ed. Mollie Lee 1969 © BBC Publications; page 8, Neil Gunn, *The Cow from The Atom of Delight*, 1956, reprinted by permission of Faber and Faber Ltd © Dairmid Gunn Esq; Page 11, Anne-Louise Verteuil and Nicola Brooks, 'Cornered' from *The Teenage Market Place* © Anne-Louise Verteuil; Page 14, William McIlvanney, 'Ah Bumped Ma Heid in the Sheuch' from *Docherty*, published by Mainstream © John Farquharson Ltd; Page 18, Norman Britton, 'No Matter How Perfect We Think We Are, We Are all Handicapped in One Way or Another' from the *Times* September 1982 © Norman Britton; Page 21, J. H. Griffin, *Black Like Me* 1964 © Collins Publishers; Page 25, Zoe Bell, 'Sexploitation' from *Payday*, May 1982 © Girobank Publications; Page 27, Carrie Carmichael, 'The Kids Today' from *Non Sexist Childraising* 1977 © Beacon Press, Boston; Page 30, the *Times* Ipswich Correspondent, June 1983, 'Family Sell Furniture to Help Tribes' © the Times Newspapers Ltd; Page 32, Roger Bush, 'Explosion' from *Prayers for Pagans* © Curtis Brown Ltd; Page 34, Sue Armstrong, 'Smoking' from *Smoking: What's in it for You?* 1977 © Macdonald Publishers; Page 38, Macdonald Hastings, *After You, Robinson Crusoe—A Practical Guide for a Desert Islander* © reprinted by kind permission of Curtis Brown Ltd on behalf of the Estate of Macdonald Hastings; Page 41, various authors, 'Capital Punishment' from the *Times* 6th July 1983 and the *Guardian* 7th and 13th July 1983 © K. H. Oldaker, former inmate of Parkhurst Prison, Mike Smith, Jenny Kirkpatrick; Page 44, H. F. Wallis, 'Reducing the Racket' from *The New Battle of Britain* © Charles Knight and Co. Ltd; Page 47, Peter Dunn, 'The Lonely Wasteland' from the *Sunday Times* 12th December 1982 © Times Newspapers Ltd; Page 50, Paul Theroux, 'Not My Kind of Place' from the *Sunday Times* 7th August 1983 © Paul Theroux; Page 53, Nadine Gordimer, 'They Danced for Joy' from *A World of Strangers* 1962 © Penguin; Page 56, Sue Arnold, 'I Vote We Have Christmas More Often' from *Living* December 1981 © *Living*; Page 59, Alison Uttley, 'Witches' from *Wild Honey* © reprinted by permission of Faber and Faber Ltd; Page 62, Lucy Berman, 'The Legend of the Kraken' from *The Creepy Crawly Book* 1973 © W. H. Allen Publishers; Page 65, Aidan Chambers, 'Wilfred Owen's Ghost' from *Great Ghosts of the World* © Pan Book Ltd; Page 68, Janet and Colin Bord, *Are We Being Watched* © Janet and Colin Bord; Page 71, Alan Burgess, 'Stop the Fighting' from *The Small Woman* © Bell and Hyman; Page 75, Harold Loukes, 'Suffering and the Nature of God' from *The Teenage Religion*—extracts from tape-recordings of classroom discussions © SCM Press Ltd; Page 78, Spike Milligan, 'Spike Milligan Protests' and 'Open Heart University' from *The Spike Milligan Letters* © Michael Joseph Ltd; Page 81, J. C. Hampe, Released from *To Die is Gain* 1978 © reprinted by permission of Darton, Longman and Todd Ltd, London; Page 84, Barbara Smoker, 'Is There A Life Hereafter' from *Humanism* © Ward Lock Educational Co. Ltd.

Jackson, Lionel
  Read and respond.
  1. English language—Examinations, questions, etc.
  I. Title II. Jackson, Mary, *1931–*
  428.2 PE1112

ISBN 0 340 37161 7

First published 1985
Second impression 1989

Printed in Great Britain for Hodder and Stoughton Educational, a division of Hodder and Stoughton Ltd, Mill Road, Dunton Green, Sevenoaks, Kent by Page Bros (Norwich) Ltd
Typeset by Macmillan India Ltd., Bangalore